From the Wilder

An Israeli Soldier's Sto

C000221299

Asael Lubotzky

FROM THE
WILDERNESS
AND LEBANON

AN ISRAELI SOLDIER'S STORY
OF WAR AND RECOVERY

TRANSLATED BY
Murray Roston

The Toby Press

From the Wilderness and Lebanon
An Israeli Soldier's Story of War and Recovery

The Toby Press LLC
POB 8531, New Milford, CT 06776–8531, USA
& POB 2455, London WIA 5WY, England
www.tobypress.com

ISBN 978-1-59264-417-9, *paperback*

A CIP catalogue record for this title is
available from the British Library

Printed and bound in the United States

In memory of Amichai Merchavia

Contents

Foreword

*Moshe (Bogie) Ya'alon**

I first met Asael Lubotzky in 2002 while I was chief of staff. At the conclusion of the annual memorial service for General Nehemia Tamari, Asael approached me, together with his father, and asked my advice concerning his upcoming mobilization, as he was hesitating between joining an elite unit or serving in an infantry regiment. After inquiring what plans, hopes, or ambitions he had for such service, I recommended that he join an infantry regiment.

Our next meeting took place in Tel Hashomer Hospital, where he was lying in bed near my nephew after both had been wounded in the Second Lebanon War. I learned there that he had in fact accepted my advice and had chosen to serve in the Golani Brigade.

Our second meeting proved to be a continuation of the first, insofar as I recognized in him a young Israeli with a sense of mission, committed to defending and strengthening his country as a national

---

* Lt. Gen. Moshe (Bogie) Ya'alon is the former IDF chief of staff and current Israeli Defense Minister.

home for the Jewish People, and endowed with a deep faith in its rightful cause. Despite the unfortunate setting and the serious injury he had suffered, I was happy to see that he had fulfilled his earlier plans by becoming an officer and educator to his fellow soldiers.

Asael's diary provides a picture of a young native-born Israeli standing up to challenges that few young men in our world are required to face: questions of life and death, of human dignity, challenges both ethical and moral, of command and operational responsibilities in peace and war and, subsequent to his injury, challenges demanding courage in overcoming pain and disabilities.

In all these respects, Asael's story proves yet again the victory of spirit over matter.

Much can be learned from reading this account by a young platoon commander serving in today's Israeli army. It will prove of value not only to other platoon commanders but also to senior officers who can obtain an insight into the world of junior officers. Moreover, those about to enter the army can learn what awaits them, while general readers will learn respect for the responsibility that rests on such young shoulders, Asael's outlook on life, his processes of thought, and his actions.

On completing my reading of the book, I felt both pride and hope for the future. In a period when we are concerned by the younger generation's tendency to avoid responsibility in general, and army service in particular, and in a period of dissatisfaction with the personal example set by our leaders, it is good to know (as I do) that there are those upon whom we can rely.

Blessed is the country that has such sons!

Introduction

This book was not planned. It grew out of personal notes jotted down while I was confined in various hospital wards. As I wrote, however, the words formed sentences, the sentences grew into paragraphs, and soon a journal began to emerge. I had originally intended the resulting journal to remain a private diary of these wartime events – one day, perhaps, I would share its contents with my children, but I had not intended it for publication. Some weeks after the war ended, I realized that certain details and events were beginning to fade from my memory, even though the associated sounds, sensations, and images remained intensely vivid. I felt compelled to organize the impressions in my mind and, as it were, lock each away in a separate drawer, isolated from my consciousness, ready to be extracted when required. The act of recording those experiences may well have helped me cope with them, for even after the war had ended, there remained my own private battle – the long period of rehabilitation. This, too, was a battle though it was vastly different fighting the enemy.

I was born in 1983, a few moments before my twin brother, Boaz, during the early months of the First Lebanon War, and grew up in the Judean town of Efrat as the eldest of six children. At the age of eighteen, after completing my studies at the local yeshiva high school Neve Shmuel, I enrolled at the Ma'ale Adumim Hesder yeshiva in the northern Judean Desert, in a program that combined religious studies with military service. In 2003, I enlisted in the Fifty-First Battalion of the Golani Brigade, a unit composed of yeshiva students. By November 2005, I had completed officers' course, and, after seven months of training with my platoon, we were mobilized to fight in the Second Lebanon War.

This book is a personal testimony, based primarily on memory. I have attempted to check facts by consulting fellow combatants from my battalion, as well as many others. However, this account makes no claim to being an objective description of my company's experiences in the Second Lebanon War, and certainly not of the entire campaign. I have tried to be faithful to the events as I experienced them, while being fully aware that it is impossible to be entirely objective, as we are all enclosed in a world of our own values, and subjective perception must necessarily leave its imprint on one's memory. This book, therefore, describes my personal perspective, the way I remember the events.

Much has been written about the Second Lebanon War. It was covered by the media in an unprecedented manner, with journalists reporting the news at dizzying speed. Though many books and articles have been published on the events of the war, I feel this book can contribute something by describing them from the point of view of a junior commander in the field. Historians with whom I have discussed the matter confirm that there exist numerous documentary records provided by senior officers, but very little documentation from soldiers and junior officers on the ground. My contribution may serve to balance the record.

Toward the end of the war, I was severely wounded. The entire book was written while I was in the process of recovery from the injuries I sustained, and I have included a description of my experiences during the many months of rehabilitation. That section was especially difficult for me to write because I could not present the events in strict order, as I did in the chapters on the fighting itself. In warfare events are terrifying and the pace is fast, whereas the rehabilitation process is mostly routine, tedious, and slow. I have tried to avoid tiresome medical descriptions, preferring to focus on the challenges of recovery. Here, perhaps even more than in the battle chapters, everything is written from my subjective point of view.

My personal acquaintance with the many fighters who fell in battle, including close friends, has created in me an urge to perpetuate their memory. Subsequent contact with the bereaved families and with the wounded has increased my desire to record the events. I hope that this book will help preserve the memory of their heroism.

Gaza

Sunday, June 25, 2006–Tuesday, July 18, 2006

Chapter One

The Assignment: Gaza

Third Platoon, silence!" Avshalom, the platoon sergeant, called to the soldiers. "No talking – Asael has an important message." The soldiers stood, listening quietly. "You've probably heard what happened this morning in Gaza. These, briefly, are the facts as far as they are known: Terrorists attacked IDF positions in southern Gaza. Some soldiers were wounded in the attack, and apparently one soldier was kidnapped and taken into the Gaza Strip. As a result of the new situation, our battalion is moving into Gaza!"

A commotion broke out among the soldiers. Most were excited at the idea: "Finally, real action – no more guard duty and patrols," "Lets bring those terrorists down," or "It's time we went there and imposed some order, the terrorism's out of control."

But there were also other voices: "Gaza? What for? What are we supposed to do – knock on the door of each house asking, 'Is there a kidnapped soldier here?'" or "What's happened to Army Intelligence? Where is the Air Force? Why should the Infantry be involved?"

There were also some disgruntled soldiers: "Just when we were due for a week's leave they push us into Gaza. Typical of the army – anything to stop us having a good time!"

Our Golani company had just completed its training course and the soldiers had received the coveted brown beret, becoming full-fledged fighters. The soldiers and officers had been expecting to enjoy a week of vacation at the army resort in Ashkelon, after which they would undergo a week's special training for battle, and take up positions on the Gaza border.

I had been sitting with Maru Gete and Achikam, the commanders of the First and Second Platoons, reviewing the course and making plans for the coming week. We had hoped to be able to relax at the resort after the pressures of the training period and, after that, to become acquainted with the other companies in the battalion. Moreover, we intended to speak personally with each of the soldiers under our command as we moved from training to operational activities, beginning Sunday, June 25, 2006.

On that Sunday morning, before leaving for the meeting point in Jerusalem, I was sitting in my parents' kitchen having breakfast, with my uniform on, my packed bag beside me, and my weapon lying on top. The radio was on in the living room but I was not listening. Suddenly, my parents entered the kitchen, my father asking in a worried voice, "Asael, have you heard what's happened?"

"No," I replied, and we turned up the volume on the radio.

The narrator announced: "Early this morning, terrorists crossed the fence in the southern Gaza Strip, attacking several targets. At least six soldiers were wounded. One has been declared missing." At the word "missing" we shuddered. "According to IDF officials, large forces are in search of the terrorists, and the incident is at present under investigation. The name of the missing soldier, who was apparently kidnapped, has not been released at this time. A number of Palestinian groups have claimed responsibility for the incident."

A soldier abducted! The doomsday scenario was upon us. For every soldier and commander, kidnapping is the most serious of events. And all this had happened in the southern Gaza Strip – the sector of which we were due to take command in a few weeks.

I recalled that the battalion was scheduled to have taken over that sector at an earlier date, but the takeover had been postponed. What would have happened had it been a member of our battalion who was kidnapped? Or one of my platoon? I tried not to think about it. My parents exchanged glances. I told them I had a feeling that my week's leave was likely to be canceled, and indeed, within a few minutes, our company commander Gal Karabaki telephoned me with the brief message: "We've been assigned to Gaza!"

The entire battalion was now moved from Jerusalem to the resort facility in Ashkelon. In the evening, an initial officers' meeting was held. Gal, who lived in the village of Ofer in the Carmel, handed out a printed summary of the incident's investigation. While waiting for the meeting to begin, I studied the text. The IDF investigation revealed that, at about 5:00 a.m., a group of seven terrorists from Gaza had infiltrated Israel via a tunnel. The terrorists had attacked three military targets near Kibbutz Kerem Shalom: an observation tower, an armored personnel carrier, and a tank. In the attack, Lieutenant Hanan Barak and Staff Sergeant Pavel Slutsker were killed, four soldiers wounded, and another soldier, Corporal Gilad Shalit, had been abducted and taken to a terrorist hideout in the Gaza Strip.

Gal opened the meeting with routine procedure, each platoon commander stating which of his men were present, who had failed to appear, and the reasons for their absence. That was normal practice, to ensure that everything was in order. However, on the day when Gilad Shalit had been abducted, the procedure carried added significance. I went through my list of soldiers, imagining that it was crying out: "Check again! Make sure everyone is here, that there's no one missing!"

Gal's voice interrupted my thoughts: "At the meeting of the company commanders, the battalion commander summarized the situation as far as it was then known. You can read the account of the abduction on your own. As regards battalion orders, nothing is yet known, but we are preparing to participate in a large-scale operation. According to the guidelines, the operation has four goals." Gal glanced down at his notebook and read them out:

- Rescuing Gilad Shalit or obtaining information of his whereabouts;
- Ending the firing of rockets at Sderot and the western Negev, as well as preventing further attacks;
- Ensuring that the terrorist organizations pay a price for having fired the rockets;
- Changing the rules of the game; namely, sending a message to the terrorist organizations that we are capable of conducting extensive operations deep inside Gaza.

Gal looked up at us, adding firmly: "It is vital to convey to your men that the basic training period is over and we are now engaged in fighting. There's no time to mess around – they must prepare themselves for going into battle. We have reached the moment of truth that we've been talking about for the last seven months."

Gete, Achikam, and I gazed at each other and knew that we could rely on the men in our company. It was true that, as in every company in the Golani brigade, there were a few soldiers with disciplinary problems, lack of motivation, or social issues, but we believed that when called upon, the soldiers would rise to the occasion and prove themselves worthy.

Thus began a month-long period of military operations and training in northern Gaza, as part of what was called "Operation Summer Rains." In the early days, orders were frequently changed. One day, Gete, Achikam, and I were studying the maps of the area. Achikam, from the town of Meḥola in the Jordan Valley, was concentrating on a map when the telephone rang. One of the squad commanders was on the line: "Achikam, is it true the operation has been postponed?"

Then came another call: "Gete, they're saying we aren't going in tonight."

This was followed by a spate of calls, all inquiring whether there had been a change of plans. Rumors were quickly spreading throughout the battalion.

Sometimes updates did not come directly to us, the officers, but filtered through from the soldiers. I called Amichai Merchavia, the commander of the Lead Platoon of the Third Rifles, who said, "Hakima, my company commander, just informed me that there is a cancellation. That's how it is in this battalion – the soldiers get to know before the officers whether the rumors are true or not."

For the first few days we stayed in the resort facility in Ashkelon (as the IDF had already paid for the week, it was decided that preparations would take place there). Later, we transferred to makeshift tents near Zikim, a permanent base. It was an area well within range of enemy rockets, and we often heard the "Red Dawn" siren (later changed to "Color Red"). Sometimes, one could even see the rockets in flight, generally toward Ashkelon.

The soldiers had brought swimwear and civilian clothes from home to wear at the resort, and were unprepared for a long period in field conditions. Avshalom, my platoon sergeant, explained to me how serious the problem was: "They were so thrilled at the prospect of a vacation that many failed to bring even a spare uniform – seems we'll be going into Gaza in our swimsuits!"

We were informed that in a few days we would be receiving assistance from the Army's Logistics Department, and indeed, one day, with sweltering heat outside and the soldiers resting in their tents, a truck turned up loaded with uniforms. As soon as the news circulated, the sleepy soldiers, in a sudden burst of energy, fell upon the goods in the truck. The soldier in charge of the truck began yelling, "Stand in two lines, each with a set of uniforms ready to exchange!" but his cries were lost in the confusion, as the men were already on the truck searching for the right-size pants and shirts. He called out, "Don't take them! Hand in the old set and you'll receive one in exchange!" but no one took any notice. Then the Master Sergeant arrived. He didn't need to raise his voice. The men immediately jumped down from the truck and stood in line: one stern glance from him and order was restored.

Living conditions were not easy in the new base camp, Zikim. The tents were crowded, the heat oppressive. Instead of being granted home leave, we remained on permanent alert at the base. However, the soldiers' motivation was high. They had been training for months, and now everyone wanted "the real experience" – action in the heart of Gaza. For many the desire for action was intertwined with the ideological motivation to defend the State.

In preparation for the operation, I called together the platoon's troops and the commanders. We sat in a small tent with maps spread out on the floor. I gave them a summary of the Intelligence reports, an analysis of the layout of the area, the goals assigned for our mission, and other classified information. The men listened intently, but what everyone was really waiting for was the moment when I would list those selected to take part in the operation. The soldiers were keen on being chosen for the fighting unit, but not all could be. The selection had to be determined by operational considerations, such as the need for a driver, a machine gunner to remain in the armored vehicle, and a medic. I read out the names of the soldiers, seeing a glint in the eye of each soldier chosen for participation while those due to stay behind showed their disappointment at missing the action, perhaps also at having had others preferred over them. Those who were assigned felt proud of being chosen because of their professional ability, and justifiably so.

My previous acquaintance with the Gaza Strip had included minor operations. Two years earlier, the battalion had been assigned responsibility for the central area, but I realized that the nature of the forthcoming operation would be different. It was not to be a matter of protecting the border fence or taking limited action, but a large-scale operation. I was a little anxious about the unknown, but hoped I would stand firm. Added to my knowledge of the territory was my familiarity with Gush Katif, the group of towns that had been destroyed a year earlier in Israel's withdrawal from Gaza. During the last year of its existence, I had often visited there and had grown to love the wind and waves of its picturesque beach. I had worked as a volunteer in the greenhouses together with its members, and later helped the evicted families transfer their belongings to temporary accommodations. I knew that in the operation before us we would come very close to the ruins of the village Dugit which had, after the evacuation, been taken over by the enemy to be used as a rocket-launching site. But that knowledge did not prepare me for the sad sight of dozens of ruined buildings and debris without a single living soul (except perhaps for terrorists), a silent witness to the flourishing community that had until recently been there.

I began to study the sector and prepare the platoon for the coming operation, receiving considerable assistance from Intelligence, including coded maps and aerial photographs of various sizes, as well as more specific aids. They were of remarkably high standard, accurate and up-to-date. I studied the maps closely to learn details of the territory, and consulted the battalion officers to determine what was to be their final route and in which buildings they intended to base themselves. The valuable support I received from them relieved me of some concerns about the operation. Many small changes needed to be made due to the input of new intelligence information, and I wanted to be sure I would set out on the mission with the latest facts. On the aerial photos, I marked in different colors the routes to be taken by the various forces, indicated the buildings due to be occupied by each platoon in the battalion, and drew on the maps the boundaries between the various battalions and companies to avoid the danger of friendly fire. Would we be able to keep strictly within these boundaries? At the planning stage, everything looks clear, but would it be possible to identify the boundaries in the dark, and under pressure?

I remembered a story concerning the boundaries of Jerusalem that I once heard from my grandfather, Iser Lubotzky, who had fought in the Golani Brigade in the War of Independence. Sitting together were Moshe Dayan (the commander of the Jerusalem district, who later became chief of the general staff and subsequently defense minister) and his Jordanian counterpart, Abdullah el-Tell. The two officers penciled in the positions of their forces. In the course of time, those lines served as the basis for dividing Jerusalem, but their inaccuracies, including the thickness of some of the penciled lines, caused numerous disputes. Who imagined that those lines would be used to define the border for a period of nineteen years, until the Six Day War? I continued marking the lines on my map, but with extra care.

During the period of our stay at Zikim, we traveled to Lachish, the Central Command training base, for training in urban warfare. On the base there, a series of buildings had been set up to simulate houses in a Palestinian street. The training involved breaking down doors. An engineering team specializing in the use of hydraulic equipment for that purpose had been assigned to teach us the technique, as the ability to break down doors quickly in order to enter a building was of major importance, since time is critical when the attacking unit is exposed to enemy fire. Unfortunately, the engineering team failed to arrive and the training was canceled.

While we were waiting for its arrival, I sat in the shade of a tree, reading a document that summarized the methods of dealing with an urban ambush, and Amichai joined me.

"What are you studying?" he asked. "Gemara or military papers?"

I smiled, remembering the period when we were soldiers in the Hesder unit, spending many hours studying together in the synagogue on Shabbat or, during the week, using texts that we carried around in our pockets.

"Guess!" I said.

Amichai continued my thoughts: "'It is a time to act for God; they have made void your Torah,'" he quoted from the Book of Psalms. "'There is a time for religious study and a time for action.'" Amichai looked over my documents, adding some helpful tips. I then gave my men a talk on the principles of urban ambush, teaching them the various stages of entry, taking up positions, waiting, and exiting, in which I stressed the tactics relevant to Gaza. The soldiers had been trained primarily to fight in the open. Now we tried to integrate rules of combat relevant to urban terrain, for example, the principle of "upward checks." In built-up territory one must not only gaze ahead down the road, but must also watch windows and roofs.

The company commanders then held a concluding exercise. The reconnaissance team advanced toward the building, while others lay undercover searching for cardboard targets. The team broke down the door and began searching the various rooms like professional counter-terrorists. The soldiers broke down door after door, shouting aloud as they did so. After careful inspection, they all entered the house and began taking up positions, stretching blankets and sheets over the windows. A group of soldiers playing the enemy suddenly launched an attack on the house. Triggers were pulled, accompanied by shouts of "Fire, fire, fire!" One of the advancing soldiers was exposed as he passed an open window. "Lie down as if wounded!" I shouted. He lay down and called, "Medic, medic!" Kobi, the medic, dragged him to shelter and bandaged his hand. Soldiers loaded him onto a stretcher. I gave the order for immediate evacuation of the house. The men swiftly left their positions, exited and began a rapid retreat, holding the stretcher aloft, to a distant point in the forest.

I was pleased with the platoon's operational level and the high motivation they revealed during these drills. I summarized the exercise: "Third Platoon, in these urban warfare drills you have demonstrated a high operational level and shown that you have grasped the basic rules. Reports from all your commanders confirm that throughout the day you worked with motivation and with determination to succeed."

We did not imagine then how much our training would help us when fighting in the North.

"Onto the buses," called Avshalom, after making sure that all the equipment had been returned in good order. In fact, to the soldiers' disappointment, we did not make use of the house-to-house tactics, as throughout our time in Gaza we were in armored vehicles.

Foot patrol or entering houses from armored vehicles is particularly dangerous and hence regarded as more exciting. Combat troops, especially early in their careers, are eager for battle, and want to mark their weapons with an "X" to indicate that they have killed a terrorist. In preparation for battle, we needed to train both soldiers and officers to fight from armored vehicles. We practiced many times equipping the vehicles, carrying over to them two stretchers loaded with gear. The first few times it took a long while for the soldiers to find where to place each item, how to insert the periscopes, where to put the cables, and how to install the observation items and the machine gun. After a few practice sessions, including changing the technique, the task became simpler and faster. We went over the printed manuals, rehearsed a series of rescue drills, and ensured that the various crew members – the drivers, gunners, and commanders – all knew their jobs.

Equally important was practicing integration with units from other corps. In the parking lot near Zikim, there were vehicles belonging to the armored corps and to the engineers. I asked their officers to provide a short practical lesson on their vehicles. The soldiers stood in a semicircle around the tank while an officer explained its capabilities and the nature of its interaction with the infantry. It was very hot, with the sun beating down. Suddenly there was a "Red Dawn" siren. "Take cover!"

Men ran for cover, sheltering beside the tanks in the vicinity. We heard the rocket explode in the distance, learning later that it had fallen near another group of soldiers, without hurting anyone, fortunately. That incident made the exercise especially meaningful.

After studying the resources of the tank, we moved across to the bulldozer. I made sure that the men knew how to force entry into the vehicles, and we practiced how to remove a casualty from them, as well as, if possible, to insert a stretcher. Inserting a stretcher into a tank or other armored vehicle full of equipment is particularly difficult. Each group practiced with its officer. Avshalom and I went around supervising the various groups and testing them, notably for speed. The objective was to perform the task as quickly as possible while ensuring no harm was caused to the wounded soldier. When the soldier acting the part of a casualty cried out that he was being hurt, those handling him were rebuked by their commanders: "Imagine if it were a real casualty! We're supposed to rescue him, not worsen his condition." How relevant these exercises were to prove during the war in the North!

The training involved wearing battle equipment in the intense heat, including the ceramic flak jacket. On firing ranges, we drilled the men in shooting under various conditions. It was important for them to become accustomed to shooting while wearing flak jackets. Sometimes, they resented the exercises, especially as the operation's objectives kept being changed.

My platoon was first assigned to the force headed by Itamar Katz, a former company commander. We formed part of the brigade's Rescue Unit, which included both heavy and light armored vehicles. The entire rescue force was under the command of Roi Klein.

I was in the tent area when Klein suddenly called me: "Asael, this is Klein! Come in five minutes to a meeting at Range Eight."

"I'm in the camp, it will take me some time to get there."

"OK, I'll pick you up," and he hung up. Although he was busy, Klein knew how to be considerate to his men. He wanted to save me the walk in the heat. As I left the tent, I could see the dust cloud raised by the jeep approaching.

Klein spoke firmly at the officers' meeting. He wanted to know the status of all forces in terms of equipment and training. However, when he pointed on a map to the location we were to take up at the beginning of the operation, he sensed a general disappointment. Like their soldiers, officers want to be deep in the field, to lead their men in a significant operation, and to have a real impact on events. Officers dislike disappointing their troops. An officer assigned a mission that is considered difficult and dangerous can inspire and motivate his men.

"I suppose you expected to be further into Gaza. I must remind you, however, that we are a rescue unit. I hope we won't be called upon, but if we are, we will perform the task to the full. You must acquaint yourselves with all operations and all routes. Who knows where we will be needed?"

Klein gave us confidence. On the one hand, I wanted to join him on the mission, but on the other hand, I preferred to be with my own men, with Company B, undertaking its own mission. In fact, the plans were changed and we were assigned a different task, my platoon being attached to the original group under Gal Karabaki.

Chapter Two

Operation "Oaks of Bashan"

O ne night, on entering a tent of the Third Rifles in search of Amichai, who was a platoon commander, I found him hunched over some maps, copying details into his notebook. I reminded him that the operation had been postponed indefinitely. "I know," he said, and explained that he wanted to be fully prepared, as one can never know how quickly things may change and how hastily we would need to undertake a new mission. Amichai recalled that during Operation Defensive Shield everything had happened rapidly, leaving little time for preparation. He felt deeply the loss of his close friend, Shmuel Weiss, who had fallen in the fighting in Jenin during Operation Defensive Shield, and wanted to be sure that he himself was fully prepared for our mission.

Only ten days later, the first operation took place, named "Oaks of Bashan." After a rocket had hit a school in Ashkelon, the government authorized an operation in the area of Al Atatra from where the rocket had been launched. It began on Thursday, July 6, ending two days later, on Saturday. It involved the entire Golani Brigade under its commander, Tamir Yadai, together with the Armored Corps, engineers, naval commandos, and other units. It was a step up in terms of activity, compared with recent years. Our company was incorporated into the Seventy-Fourth Battalion of the Armored Corps.

Before the operation, there was an exchange of information at brigade level, directed by the commander of the Golani Brigade, and watched by the commander of the Gaza Division, Aviv Kochavi, and GOC Southern Command, Yoav Galant. One by one, the unit commanders came forward and explained their plans, from the brigade commander to the battalion and company commanders. In preparation for the operation, we visited a number of observation posts, some on the border fence, some further away that required special instruments for surveillance. I was standing with Achikam and Gete in one of the posts when a Givati soldier, looking bored, turned to us and asked, "Who are you? Do you belong to the Golani operation?"

When he realized we were platoon commanders of the November 2005 group, he was amazed. "What! Is the November '05 group moving into Gaza?" We nodded. It was hard not to smile at the envious look he gave us. It was as if we were talking of some dream vacation overseas. The soldier obviously did not know it, but later on, the Golani and Givati brigades would hold alternate operations in Gaza. We comforted him by informing him that his brigade was scheduled to take over at the end of the Golani Brigade's operations.

I raised my binoculars and gazed at the sand dunes. A desert! "Do you remember when we were here last summer?" said Gete. Maru Gete and I had studied together at yeshiva before our enrollment. We had joined together, and had shared many experiences in recent years. I recognized the ruins of the village Dugit. It was sad to return to a place where we had walked around so freely in the past, and now come to it armed and in heavily armored vehicles.

On the night of the operation, the entire battalion reached a point adjacent to the border crossing into northern Gaza. Klein moved vigorously among the vehicles to ensure that they were all in their correct places. Each vehicle had been assigned a special flag, sprayed onto a piece of canvas hanging at the side. In that way, we were able to identify who was in the vehicle by the number and letter beneath the tactical markings. We waited on the firing range at the base camp, Zikim, checking finally that all was in order, including the equipment. I zipped up my laces firmly. I felt that everything was ready. We had waited a long time for this operation, the soldiers were well-trained, the equipment had been tested and was in good condition.

My men were seated along the walls of the firing range, the tension and excitement overcoming their fatigue. A gentle breeze caressed our faces, easing the heat. I listened to the sounds coming from the nearby range. The battalion commander of the Armored Corps was speaking of the army's fighting spirit. I wondered what final remarks I should make to my soldiers before entering Gaza: to discuss the general purpose of fighting or focus on details? I chose the first option.

"I want to concentrate on two aspects," I told them. "First, our mission; namely, that we have been sent to defend our country, its citizens in general and the residents of the region that was attacked by rockets in particular, as well as to help toward the release of Gilad Shalit. The second is our readiness for the mission. We have undergone long training for this operation. This is the moment for us to gather all our strength, and to act calmly and professionally. I rely on you to do the job."

With these words I tried to allay the soldiers' fears, but it seemed that their suppressed excitement had banished all sense of fear. There was noisy commotion around us, indicative of the final pressures before our departure on our mission. We boarded the armored vehicle and checked that everything was in order.

There was a call on the field telephone: "Is that Bungalow Three? Sergeant One here!"

"Bungalow Three here, what do you want?"

"What about *Tefillat HaDerekh* ('Prayer Before Setting Out on a Journey')?"

"You're right! One minute."

I reached into my pocket, retrieved my small prayer book, and switched on the company's communication system. "Bungalow Three here. I'm about to say *Tefillat HaDerekh*":

May it be the divine will to lead us out toward peace, to direct our footsteps toward peace, to guide us toward peace. May You bring us to our destination for life, joy, and peace, and permit us to return in peace. Save us from the hand of all enemies, ambushes, bandits, and wild animals on the way, and from all kinds of punishments that may come to the world. Send blessing in all that we do, and grant us favor, kindness, and mercy, both in Your eyes and in the eyes of all who see us. Hear the sound of our entreaties, for You are God, who hears prayers and entreaties. Blessed are You, Hashem, who hears prayer.

Every word took on added significance on leaving for battle. We could only pray that we would all return safely.

The operation began with a raid from the sea by navy commandos (Shayetet Thirteen), who took over the Gaza Strip's casino. Intelligence had discovered that armed terrorists had barricaded themselves inside it. After killing the terrorists, the commandos established an observation post on the top floor of the casino in order to help ground forces take up positions in the area. Soon, mobile forces from our battalion began setting up urban ambushes in the town of Al Atatra. Our company's role was to open up the coastal axis along the Gaza coast, the so-called "Tranquil" axis leading from north to south and ending at the casino, a few kilometers south of the border fence.

We crossed through the gate of the electrified fence, forming a long column along the sand paths. Two bulldozers, with their blades to the ground to remove landmines, led our force through a path a blade-and-a half wide. Army Intelligence believed that the path had been mined at several points. Behind the bulldozers came the company commander on a raised vehicle providing the advantage of improved vision and permitting overall command. We, the remaining company's commanders and our men, followed in armored vehicles. Our company possessed a heavily armored combat engineering vehicle and armored personnel carrier that contained a device for breaking through obstacles; it could fire fueled rockets that exploded on the ground, their impact setting off any mines in the area. In that way, a path a hundred meters long could be created, wide enough for our vehicles to travel along.

We reached the area of suspected mines and halted. The sound of the sea was lost in the deafening roar of the engines, though we could still hear the sound of firing in the distance. Gal announced on the company's radio: "Bungalow Unit Commander speaking. Confirm that you hear me!" After all units had confirmed, Gal announced: "In a few moments the Grays will open up the route with its special device," – that is, the Engineering Corps with its gray berets would fire its special device.

We closed up all hatches in our vehicle, and I prepared the men for nearby explosions. Through our periscopes, we watched intently what was happening. After a few moments, the missiles were fired and we observed their semicircular flight. Boom! There was a huge, deafening explosion. Our vehicle shook, and seemed about to lift off the ground despite its substantial weight. The device had achieved its goal: if there were mines, they had no doubt exploded along with the missile. But, unexpectedly, the launching caused a fire in the engine of the combat engineering device. The engineers tried to extinguish it but it had been permanently disabled. A bulldozer came to remove the failed apparatus, despite the protests of its crew.

During entry into Gaza, we fired numerous rounds from our machine gun, the men being excited at their first experience of shooting in a combat situation. I remembered my first combat experience in Palestinian territory, how the sound of gunfire and the smell of gunpowder mingled with the excitement and tension.

We encountered several positions held by the Palestinian police and we raked them until we were sure that the area had been cleared. The soldiers squeezed the trigger as they had in training, only this time the targets were not made of cardboard. We had no idea if the positions were manned or empty. Had we killed anyone? No one asked the question and no one went to check. If there really were terrorists there, we were happy that it was they who were killed and not us.

After traveling along the opened road, we settled into defensive positions. Around us, on the sandy soil, there were low-growing shrubs. Behind, to the west, naval boats protected us from terrorists trying to sneak ashore. In front were gray stone houses, crowded together, their windows facing us. Some of them had walled compounds. Each window could be concealing a sniper, and terrorists could emerge from any of the houses.

I divided up the observation area with the other units, and established common terms for reporting and identifying circuits of fire. "Is that 1B? Bungalow Three here. Let us establish common terms," I called to the tank commander.

"1B here to receive the terms," he replied.

I continued, "Boundary left, the building with the antenna, to be referred to as Antenna. To the right, a group of houses surrounded by a green fence to be referred to as Green. Do you hear me, 1B?"

"I hear you!"

"To the right of the green fence, a few hundred meters along, can you see some ruined houses?" I didn't wait for a reply. "They are the ruins of the village Dugit to be referred to as…" There was a moment's silence as I hesitated. "…the village Dugit," I concluded. A sense of loss accompanied those words. Here, what had been until a year ago a village standing proudly on its hill had become merely a point for surveillance.

In a defensive situation, battle order has to be maintained in the vehicle: the duty roster for surveillance and security, ensuring alertness, exercises for responding to various situations, awareness of the shared language, extinguishing lights at night, and preserving cleanliness within the vehicle. To recharge the batteries, we switched on the engine for ten minutes every hour.

At dawn, I woke the men for morning parade. The period of drowsiness is the most dangerous. Only after the sun rose did I lower the level of alertness to the norm, allowing some of the men to sleep. I called for a brief check of equipment. Everyone inspected his personal equipment. I took special care that each one checked that his grenades were in place and in correct order.

"Have you checked your grenades?" I asked one soldier as he climbed down from the gunner's position. He put his hand into his protective jacket, and fumbled inside, reaching for the grenade holder. Then he pulled out the grenade, holding it like a glass of wine over a white cloth. "Turn it over, with the handle toward your body," I reminded him, helping him to return it to its place. I noticed that his hand was cold and sweaty, and I too thought for a moment of the grenade's explosive power.

I recalled the time when I was training recruits to handle grenades. The soldiers entered the testing area one by one. I waited there, wearing my flak jacket, helmet, and goggles. Each soldier received a grenade from the sergeant and took up his position. I could see the tension in the way they walked, careful not to trip and – Heaven forbid! – drop the grenade. I recalled the safety briefing before entering the range. Before throwing a live grenade, each soldier would throw a dummy grenade that simulated the drawing of the pin and produced a small explosion. I practiced the drill with every soldier and deliberately dropped a dummy grenade on the floor. We all yelled: "There's a grenade!" A soldier ran outside and took cover. I followed and lay on top of him. The rule is for an officer to protect his men with his own body. How easy in a practice session, and how difficult under live conditions, I thought to myself.

We remained in the vehicle for many long hours. It consisted of an armored personnel carrier fitted onto the base of a captured Soviet tank whose turret had been removed. I looked around: boxes of ammunition in their holders, along with boxes of reserve field rations. Fire extinguishers placed on the shelf, due to function automatically if fire broke out. Wires dangling from above and, between them, air ducts aimed toward the crew. Our helmets connected by cables to the radio equipment. The color had faded long ago on the metal seats and the folding bench. In front, to the left, sat the driver, leaning over the steering wheel and surrounded by various dials. To the right, the gunner slumped over the periscope. A belt of machine-gun ammunition dangled down, connected to the gun. A dim light entered through the periscopes. Water bottles rolled around the floor. The original tidiness had been relaxed for the comfort of the soldiers sprawled over the floor. A pile of large bags was stacked at the back, one containing food, with snacks added by the soldiers. Another held equipment for break-ins. Avshalom, the sergeant, had crammed into the bags everything that could be useful in due course, from reserve batteries to rolls of toilet paper. At the back of the vehicle, near the massive engine, was the exit ramp to the electric elevator. There, too, a soldier was on duty, looking through a slit to prevent us from being surprised from behind. Seven soldiers located inside a steel box designed to preserve our lives!

During the day we heard that a soldier in the Thirteenth Battalion had been seriously wounded. We had not heard details and hoped for the best. We were told to isolate the area to prevent terrorists exploiting the situation. After dividing up the firing sectors, we shot for quite a long time at the open spaces between the houses. By doing so, we hoped to deter terrorists from leaving their hiding places to attack rescue crews. Our massive fire, especially that of the tanks, apparently achieved its purpose, as we saw no attempt to move between the buildings. Exchanges of fire continued, but they were distant. Even when we were shot at, the firing was inaccurate and from light weapons, incapable of penetrating the vehicle's armor plating.

After about thirty hours, we left Gaza, driving to the fence in order to refuel and to deal with any problems. During a maneuver, a tank had rubbed against one of our vehicles, manned by Emmanuel, the deputy company commander, and Sergeant Avshalom. It was only after we climbed down from our vehicles that we discovered that a piece of armor plating had been dislodged, exposing the side. The repair crew worked hard, with our help, trying to fix the vehicle, but the damage could not be repaired in so short a time. It was decided that for the return journey, Emmanuel would join my vehicle, leaving Avshalom and his crew with the vehicle that was being repaired. Additional rations, water, and ammunition were supplied. We waited near the fence for a while. It was a few hours before dusk and the onset of Shabbat. I contacted Rabbi Rabinovich, the head of Ma'ale Adumim Yeshiva, where I had studied.

"Hello! This is Asael, a past student. May I speak to the rabbi?" I glanced at my watch. "I apologize for telephoning at this hour but I am calling from the army." I hesitated to give further details.

"Yes, the rabbi will speak to you."

A few moments later: "Hello Asael, how are you? Where are you calling from?"

"Hello, Rabbi, how are you? Thank Heaven, I'm fine. I'm at the Gaza Strip fence. We have just left an operation in Gaza and are due to return there before Shabbat."

"May God protect you, both coming and going. What did you want? Is everything all right?"

"Thank Heaven, everything is fine. I wanted to ask you how the rules of Shabbat apply in the various situations we may encounter there."

"Soldiers operating in the heart of Gaza? You must in all situations behave as if it were a normal weekday, on the principle that 'saving life cancels out all Shabbat prohibitions.' Concentrate on your army duties. The Torah says: '*Live* by the laws of the Torah; don't die by them!' May Heaven protect you and return you unscathed." The rabbi's words were encouraging.

We returned to the Gaza Strip on Friday night, and held a shortened version of the Shabbat evening prayers. I took my Siddur out of my kitbag, and the men crowded around, attempting to read the small print by the dim light entering through the vehicle's slits. Those on duty hummed softly as we began reciting the prayers. There were seven men in the vehicle, each with a different tradition of prayer. Most soldiers do not pray on weekdays, but Shabbat is different. All felt united during those few moments, welcoming in Shabbat. Together we intoned the well-known song: "Come let us greet Shabbat, the bride." And thus we welcomed it in.

I behaved as on a weekday, but I wanted some reminder that it was Shabbat. When I wanted to know the time, I didn't light up my watch dial, but held the watch close to the dashboard, reading the time by its light. It was only a small change, but it helped remind me that today was Shabbat.

Early next morning, we received orders to advance. The units moved out in formation, carefully covering each other. We were the last to leave at dawn. The operation achieved most of its objectives, dozens of militants were killed, and our forces performed well. But the success was overshadowed by a serious operational failure. Yehuda (Udi) Basel from the Thirteenth Battalion was killed by friendly fire. He was the one we had heard of as seriously wounded, but he did not survive his injury. I thought how much training we had undergone in order to prevent such incidents, and no doubt the Thirteenth Battalion had done the same, yet how difficult it was to avoid. Apart from that, a few soldiers had been lightly wounded.

After we returned to the base camp at Zikim, a number of senior officers came to congratulate us and to encourage us. The battalion's soldiers sat on benches in a makeshift dining room, having already had showers to remove the layers of dirt and sweat from their bodies. Asor, the commander of the Fifty-First Battalion, spoke first, followed by Tamir, the commander of the Golani Brigade, and then Kochavi, the divisional commander. I don't remember what everyone said, but I do remember that Kochavi began with the order: "Stand up anyone who has managed to kill a terrorist!"

A number of soldiers stood up hesitantly. Others, who had not stood, were nudged by their companions till they too stood up. Kochavi turned to one of them and said: "Tell us what happened, and what weapon the terrorist had."

"The truth is, he wasn't exactly armed," said the soldier, shifting nervously. There was a hush in the audience.

The commander gave him a piercing look. "So why did you shoot him?"

"It was an anti-tank unit. The terrorist I shot was directing the fire, but he was not himself armed."

There was a burst of laughter. Of course, every anti-tank squad endangers us and each member is considered armed. His words became a subject for jokes: "The truth is he was not exactly…" "I didn't exactly shoot him…" "I didn't exactly hit him…" and so forth.

The battalion was feeling very good, and motivation had increased.

Chapter Three

Operation "Final Score"

We worked hard to prepare for the next operation, attempting to learn from the previous one and to optimize training for the future. On Wednesday, July 12, in a makeshift briefing room, our company officers held a meeting with those of the Seventy-Fourth Battalion's Armored Corps to which we had been assigned. Suddenly, the intelligence officer entered and whispered something to the battalion commander. The latter's expression indicated that something serious had occurred. I exchanged glances with Gete. An officer whispered that his wife had left a message saying she had heard there was trouble in the North. Mobile phones began beeping. The commander interrupted the whispering: "Attention! This morning, contact was lost with a Lebanese border patrol. Northern Command has declared an emergency. There are reports of the kidnapping of soldiers, but the reports have not been confirmed. Meanwhile, we will continue to plan the operation in Gaza. We'll update you if there are any changes." The harsh news was confirmed a few hours later, with the publication of the official list.

I returned to camp. Rumors were rife. Soldiers tried to obtain information from their parents who had access to the Internet and other media. The next day we heard the official report of the incident. Soldiers crowded around the radio as the announcer described what had happened:

"Yesterday morning, at 9:00 a.m., a terrorist squad broke through the fence in the area of Zar'it, entered Israeli territory and, with anti-tank missiles and small-arms fire, attacked two military vehicles that were patrolling the border. The terrorists killed three Israeli soldiers who were in one vehicle, and abducted two Israeli reservists from the Fifth Brigade of the IDF, Ehud Goldwasser and Eldad Regev. The terrorists retreated to Lebanon with the two hostages. Northern Command has declared a high emergency. An IDF tank that entered Lebanon to rescue the soldiers hit a mine and its four crew members were killed. In the attempt to extract the bodies from the tank, another soldier was killed by sniper fire. At the same time, Ḥezbollah opened up a heavy barrage aimed at Israeli towns and at IDF outposts in the area."

The army responded with a massive air strike accompanied by artillery fire. Ground forces did not participate in the first stage, as the army wished to avoid ground battles with the enemy. We were kept informed of the situation in the North, and heard that the Air Force was in control of the area.

I recalled an exercise when I was in a squad commanders' course. We had trained for a number of days, concluding with a demonstration watched by a large group, including senior officers from headquarters. Planes and helicopters took part in that exercise, bombing various targets and dropping supplies to the troops. Upon asking why the Air Force did not participate in all such exercises, we received two replies: First of all, the cost of operating the aircraft was very high. Secondly, the Air Force did not need exercises – just call them and they'd do the job.

I was hoping that the Air Force would use its air superiority to cause heavy damage to Ḥezbollah. We were told to continue our activities in Gaza as normal.

Rumors began circulating among the men. What was the Golani Brigade going to do? Would we remain in Gaza? Perhaps we would go up north? The more knowledgeable soldiers explained their views: "The Golani Brigade belongs to the Northern Division and operates in the North. They can't enter Lebanon without the Golani."

Others claimed, "GOC Southern Command will not release the Golani. We've been training for Gaza, we're here and ready for action. They'll use other brigades."

We had no idea what was going to happen. They badgered me with questions, but I told them that I had only the media to rely on. Now we had to focus on preparing for action in Beit Ḥanoun.

The day after the kidnapping was the Fast of Tammuz. The Mishna in Taanit enumerates five events that had occurred in the past on the seventeenth day of that month: the breaking of the Tablets at Mt. Sinai, the cancellation of the daily sacrifice in the Temple, the breaking down of the walls of Jerusalem, the burning of the Torah, and the placing of an idolatrous image in the Temple. That day marks the beginning of the three weeks of mourning leading to the date of the Temple's destruction on the 9th of Av. The rabbis recommended special care during that period as it is traditionally connected with disasters. On the previous day, we had suffered a serious setback in the North and we prayed that it would not prove a bad omen for what was to follow.

Although we were fasting, we continued our preparations. I abstained from eating, but the intense heat convinced me that I would have to drink in order to be ready for action and to avoid dehydration. I sipped a little water. A soldier from a traditional family saw me and asked incredulously, "Aren't you fasting?"

"I would like to fast, but I have to drink to be prepared for action," I replied. I explained to him that operational needs supersede religious laws, even if the operation itself has not yet begun. Preparations are critical for the success of a mission. Moreover, there is a danger of dehydration if we don't drink during the day.

As mentioned, there were many operational changes, mainly a series of twenty-four-hour postponements. Once again, we were not surprised that the action in Beit Ḥanoun was being delayed until the situation in the North had become clearer. We already knew the details of the operation, but did not know on which night it would begin. Then, at last, Operation Final Score was approved.

We entered the town of Beit Ḥanoun on Saturday night, July 16. The old College of Agriculture there was being used as a rocket-launching site; jokingly we remarked that one of the basic courses being taught there was ballistics.

Our platoon was to consist of two armored vehicles, so I was able to send one crew home. However, during Shabbat, the Operations Officer informed us that we could use an additional vehicle, so I had to recall Uri's crew from home leave. We equipped the vehicle in preparation but the crew did not manage to reach us in time, arriving just after we left. At first, I was disappointed, feeling that recalling them on Shabbat had all been in vain, but later I realized that perhaps it was all for the best. Everything now was performed under pressure. Even though they had participated in all the preparations until then, their being on leave may have lowered the level of their effectiveness.

We left as a column of armed vehicles. Two bulldozers led the force, followed by a tank containing the company commander. After that came my vehicle, then that of my sergeant, Avshalom, with a further tank bringing up the rear. When we were a few hundred meters from the "Spinner" neighborhood (a neighborhood in Beit Ḥanoun that, in aerial photos, looked like a child's spinning top), the tank company's commander ordered me to take up a position together with the bulldozer and the other tank, to provide covering fire for the area. I pulled to the left to allow Avshalom to pass me and join the company commander. Avshalom drove on for a short way but suddenly lost sight of the commander's tank. As he could not see the path ahead, he halted and asked for guidance. Then he saw the bulldozer and the commander's tank a few meters in front of him, but, in attempting to straighten out, his vehicle toppled into a trench five meters deep, and overturned. The company commander tried to contact him: "Bungalow Three Sergeant! Bungalow Three Sergeant!" but to no avail.

I tried to reach him on another frequency. No answer – only silence. After a short and anxious wait, I tried his mobile phone, but it was not functioning. However, I managed to make contact with the mobile phone of another crew member. I heard shouting and noise, and asked to speak with Avshalom. Avshalom came on the line and quietly informed me that they had indeed overturned but all were conscious, and he was checking for injuries. I immediately alerted the rescue team, and passed on the information.

While awaiting the arrival of the deputy commander of the Seventy-Fourth Armored Battalion, which was due to rescue the injured, we raked the Spinner neighborhood with fire. Our main fear was that terrorists would exploit the situation. Mor and Idan, who were the most severely injured, were removed on stretchers, transferred to a tank ambulance containing a medical team, and then taken back to Israel.

Avshalom and Michael, the squad commander, together with Shai, Gabi, and Shahar, took cover behind their vehicle until it was pushed upright by the bulldozer. A mechanic arrived, inspected it, and decided that, despite its loss of oil, it was capable of being driven back out of the Gaza Strip. As its machine gun had been crushed, depriving the crew of the ability to defend itself, they were escorted back by a tank, the injured soldiers being transferred to Barzilai Hospital, in Ashkelon.

In a later investigation of the incident, it was found that, while the company commander had identified the trench to the left, Avshalom had possessed less sophisticated night-vision goggles and therefore did not see the danger. He had also received no warning. This was the first time a vehicle of this type had overturned. The event aroused considerable interest in the units that used it and we received calls asking for further details. The driver, Mor, had suffered a broken neck, underwent surgery at Tel Hashomer hospital, and began the process of rehabilitation. Idan had torn a knee ligament and required physical therapy. Shai, Gabi, and Shahar had suffered bruises and cuts and, after a few days' home rest, returned to duty.

While we remained in the defensive position, I exercised the men in accuracy of fire. The goal was to create a fire deterrent to prevent the enemy from approaching our vehicles. I used a laser designator whose beam was only visible through night goggles. I also gave Ohad, the gunner; Benizri, the light machine gunner; and Costa and Omri, the sharpshooters, practice in tracking a moving target and, when given permission, providing accurate fire. The light machine gunner, using his night sight, followed the target, and fired whenever I gave him a light tap on his helmet. Part of the training was to learn how to conserve ammunition and to fire only when on target. For the machine gunner, the limit on ammunition was not significant as we had dozens of boxes aboard. The bursts of gunfire penetrated our earplugs. We required our sharpshooters only to fire when on target.

During the operation, the bulldozers, escorted by armored vehicles and tanks, leveled many areas, removing the shrubs that had been used as cover for rocket-launching squads. Numerous terrorists streamed into the area, many of them being hit by IAF helicopters before they could engage our ground forces. Some of them managed to reach the area of the College and were killed by fire both from our armored vehicles and from our snipers hidden in the buildings.

The operation took about sixty hours and we exited early on Tuesday morning, July 18. The objectives had been achieved, large areas had been cleared of brush, and many terrorists killed. But the launching of rockets at the western Negev did not end. Even though no one had imagined that our operation would stop the rockets, we were disappointed when we heard of further attacks. And of course, Gilad Shalit remained in captivity.

Each company received a two-day home leave. That night, I went directly to Tel Hashomer hospital to visit Mor. It was hard for me, as an officer, to visit an injured soldier from my unit, as I felt a sense of responsibility. At the hospital, I realized what a miracle had occurred, the doctors reporting that the broken vertebra was only millimeters away from the spinal cord. Mor was eventually able to walk and function normally, albeit with pain, but he was spared being paralyzed. Then I visited Shai, injured mainly in the face. It was swollen and full of cuts, but his eyes smiled at me, a smile that was infectious. I was proud of my men. Their injuries had not broken their spirit, which remained strong.

Late at night, my cell phone rang. Gal, the company commander, was on the line. "We're off to the North," he said briefly. "I have no further information," was his reply to my question. "We'll talk in the morning. Make sure that all your men receive the message," and he hung up.

Moving up north? To Lebanon? I had never been in Lebanon. They said Ḥezbollah had been preparing for this moment for years. I tried to remember the lectures on the enemies' forces that we had heard in our officers' course. I could not organize my thoughts. And what about our equipment? Who would transport it? Where, really, would we be going? Fatigue finally took its course. It looked like I'd need those hours of sleep.

Lebanon

Wednesday, July 19, 2006–Wednesday, August 9, 2006

Chapter Four

Preparing for Battle

Wednesday, July 19, 2006–Saturday, July 22, 2006

On the Wednesday morning following Gal's announcement that we were going north, we established contact with everyone in our unit to ensure they were all ready. I managed to look in on Ben who was suffering from a cracked rib, and paid a short visit to my yeshiva at Ma'ale Adumim, where I had studied before joining the army. Together with friends, I had spent many hours there engaged in various aspects of Jewish learning: Talmud, Jewish law, Bible, ethics, philosophy, and more. I met with a number of the rabbis in the beit midrash, who wished me luck and a safe return, and, before leaving, I briefly passed on to my friends what information I had. As I hurried down the stairs, I passed by someone, failing to notice who it was. "Asael!" he called, "Where are you rushing off to?"

I recognized that it was the friend I had always studied with. "Sorry, I didn't see you! I'm off to the army."

"Are you still in Gaza?"

"We were yesterday. Tomorrow we're leaving for the North."

"To Lebanon?" He grew serious. He was a few years older than I; he must have been there during his military service, I thought.

"Lebanon," he said again. "I've quite a few memories from there – some good, some less so. But this is no time for nostalgia." He tapped me on the shoulder and said, "Keep cool! Take care of yourself."

"And of my soldiers," I added, and hurried off.

That night I worked on the computer, listening to the familiar sounds of the home of my sleeping family, the door closed, the wind blowing through the trees outside. I searched the computer databases for information on Lebanon, on Hezbollah, and on the security zone. Although I knew I would receive military briefings before the mission, it was important to get to know as well as possible the concepts and historical background of the area. I stuffed into my backpack some hiking maps of the North, along with a road atlas I happened to possess.

The next day, Thursday, we traveled to the Northern Command training base at Elyakim for a briefing before the ground incursion into Lebanon. There were a few preparatory lectures on intelligence matters and on Hezbollah. A lecturer explained that Hezbollah ("The Party of Allah") is an Islamic Shi'ite organization active in Lebanon, its military activity focused on guerrilla and terrorist operations against Israel. After Israel's withdrawal from southern Lebanon in 2000, Hezbollah had built outposts along the border, accumulated weapons, and trained its men for a second confrontation. The fighting tactics of the terrorists were studied through videos showing them in action, and there were computer presentations. Arsenals of weapons and ammunition held by the organization were displayed, the kind of explosives used, and the nature of their camouflage. The information we received removed some of our concerns, but not all. At noon, we left to engage in field exercises until night.

During the exercises, rumors began to spread about an attack on the Egoz Commando Unit in the village of Maroun A-Ras. This came only a day after the Maglan Unit had suffered a number of casualties in a clash with terrorists. We waited with our kitbags at the meeting point. The men took drinks and lined up to refill their bottles from the jerry cans. I stood in line along with members of another company. The sun had set and my shoulder rank could not be seen in the dark. I listened to their conversations.

"Did you hear what happened to Egoz? The moment they crossed the fence, they were attacked, and a number of them were wounded," said one, lifting the jerry can.

His friend held his bottle under the can and added, "Hezbollah's expecting us. If Egoz, that was specially trained to fight in Lebanon, was caught out, what will happen to us? How can we be assigned to Lebanon when we know nothing about it?" After he had filled his bottle, it was my turn, and I could see the anxiety in the eyes of the soldier holding the jerry can.

The rumors were soon confirmed, causing considerable concern throughout the battalion. There was increased disquiet when it was discovered that one of those killed was the company commander, Benji Hillman. His brother, Shimon, was a deputy company commander of the Auxiliary Company of the Fifty-First Battalion, and Benji himself had served in a previous appointment as commander of the Third Rifles in our battalion. Many officers and soldiers asked to attend the funeral, but, under the circumstances, it was not possible to allow all of them to go.

We spent the rest of the time improving our equipment, holding inspections, and making final preparations. On Shabbat, the battalion was due to move to the Golani training base at Regavim, as we needed to make room for mobilized reserve units that were to occupy the Elyakim base. Just before dark and the onset of Shabbat, I drove to Camp Shraga, the main base of the Golani Brigade near Nahariya, to receive my orders. I was the only officer from the company, my platoon having been assigned to a group composed of infantry and members of the Tank Corps.

At Camp Shraga, I heard the plans for the operation, according to which the battalion was to take over the village of Taibeh to the west of Metula, in the framework of the 162nd Division under Brigadier General Guy Tzur. Later, the plan was changed to the nearby village of Rab A-Taltin.

I happened to be sitting with Tamir Yadai, the commander of the Golani Brigade; Ofek Buchris, the incoming commander of the Three Hundredth Brigade (who was also wearing a brown beret, as he was a former member of the Golani Brigade); and the battalion commanders of Golani. As the intelligence officer spread out the maps and aerial photos on the table, everyone crowded around. I was impressed that preparations had reached so advanced a stage, with senior officers having planned the operation down to the last detail.

During Shabbat, I met many friends from the Reconnaissance Battalion of the Golani Brigade, who were also busy preparing for the operation. Friends from Gush Etzion and high school, Danny Friedler and Gabi Grabin, hosted me in their compound. Both were officers in the Engineers and Demolition Unit. We talked about the operations in Gaza.

"Hey, was it one of your platoon's vehicles that flipped over in Beit Ḥanoun?" Danny asked.

"Yes, it was my sergeant's."

"But they say that that type of vehicle can't overturn," commented an interested bystander.

"We haven't had much luck with them. Were you in one throughout the campaign?" asked Gabi.

"Like sardines in a can. I know Gaza mostly through a slit or through the periscope," I replied.

"Couldn't you put your head out while traveling?"

"No," I replied.

"Actually, I don't do that either," he confessed, "but Elkabetz, our company commander, used to put his head out even when close to buildings. He claimed that if the Arabs wanted to kill him, they had already had ample opportunity…"

Elkabetz's real purpose was to be able to survey the area and command his force more effectively. I thought that maybe in some situations it would be right to put out one's head.

I saw a group of medics undergoing a refresher course in preparation for entering Lebanon. The atmosphere was tense and the medics tried to defuse the tension with bursts of laughter, recalling amusing incidents when they were aiding the injured.

"Remember Shlomi, who was always scratching himself? On every journey, he used up my supply of talc."

"I once took care of someone who had slipped six meters during a rope-climbing exercise. The friction had burned the palms of his hands, removing almost all the skin." Some medics shivered at the description, others recalled worse situations that had occurred during their training.

In due course, the operation was again changed, and all the plans we had worked on were shelved. After several further changes, it was decided that we would attack the town of Bint Jbeil in a full-division raid. The Golani Brigade was placed under the Ninety-First Division, the "Galilee Division," commanded by Brigadier-General Gal Hirsch. The plan was to surround the town with three brigades. The Golani and the Paratroopers would create a pincer movement, with the Golani to the east and the Paratroopers to the west, and the Seventh Armored Brigade would seize control of the areas south of the town. The operation was planned to take forty-eight hours. There was also talk of continuing northward and raiding the terrorist hideouts near the village of Kunin. My platoon was assigned to work with the main company.

On Saturday afternoon, Gal sent a car to take me to Camp Shraga. I stopped off at the base camp, Elyakim, to pick up my *tefillin* that I had left in the synagogue – the phylacteries that an Orthodox Jew places on his arm and head each morning. I decided not to be without them as long as it lay in my power, recalling how Rabbi Haim Sabato, a teacher at Yeshivat Ma'ale Adumim, told how he had put on his *tefillin* every day, even in the midst of fighting during the Yom Kippur War. In fact, my *tefillin* accompanied me throughout the war, wherever I was, placed in the pocket or back pouch of my flak jacket.

In the evening, I prayed in the synagogue together with dozens of mobilized reservists. During Shabbat, I wondered what the reservists were doing here. They looked as if they had been dragged away from civilian life. They did not look like a unit ready for combat, and kept complaining of lack of equipment and lack of operational readiness. In contrast, we "regulars" were better organized; we had all of our equipment, and were freshly trained. On the other hand, we had never been on Lebanese soil, while the reservists had accumulated considerable experience in fighting there. Although we were better prepared, equipped and trained, I felt we were going into the unknown.

It was time for *Havdala,* the prayer marking the end of
Shabbat:

> Behold, God is my salvation. I will trust and not be afraid,
> for the Lord, God, is my strength and song. Draw water while
> rejoicing, from the springs of salvation. Salvation is God's, may
> Your blessing be upon Your people. Blessed are You, God, who
> separates between the holy and profane, between light and
> darkness, between Israel and the nations, between the seventh
> day and the six days of creation.

I didn't realize then how different Shabbat would be from the coming weekdays.

I left to join my men at the Golani base, Regavim.

Chapter Five

Operation "Steel Web"

Sunday, July 23, 2006–Friday, July 29, 2006

"You know, I shouldn't really be here." I looked up from the map and saw that our driver was waiting for a response. "Why, where should you be?" I asked. It was noon on Sunday, and we were on our way up to the northern town of Avivim. That morning, we had managed to make final adjustments to our vehicle, and were now on our way to Lebanon.

"Me? I'm supposed to be on my way to Ashkelon, but the driver assigned to you skipped off, claiming he was sick." Our driver, it seems, didn't believe the fellow's story. Many drivers, he explained, avoided shuttle trips to the North because of the rocket attacks. "Why did you agree, then?" I asked. He replied: "If you don't do the job, how will it get done? If I don't drive you, how can you do it?"

We were traveling along a road packed with army vehicles, tank transporters, and army trucks. There was very little civilian traffic. We passed artillery batteries firing incessantly, command vehicles loaded with antennae, and parking lots crowded with troops preparing to leave for battle. There were flashes in the sky, which was filled with trails marking the flight of the shells. The northern towns were remarkably quiet, the forests and agricultural lands in flames. Explosions pierced the silence of the night, but we had not yet learned to distinguish between the sounds of our gunfire and the explosion of enemy shells. As we passed through the forest, we could see the battalion's other companies preparing for the operation. Preparations were hurried, because the mission had been moved up a day. We drove to the gathering point for heavy vehicles near a kibbutz. I did not know precisely where to park and tried calling Karabaki: "Karabaki, where am I supposed to park? Do you know where we are supposed to be?" But there was no response and I hung up. The communications network assigned to officers and NCOs had become overloaded, and had collapsed.

We picked up a tanker who needed a ride from his kibbutz to the meeting point. "You want to know where to park? Actually, I saw some vehicles like yours just ahead of you." We parked on the roadside beside two other vehicles. The area was full of tanks and heavy trucks. Hundreds of soldiers were running around in all directions. Where were the rest of the armored vehicles? How could anyone find anything in all this mess? I suddenly felt like a small cog in a machine in need of oiling.

Our men climbed out and began unpacking equipment while Avshalom made sure that everything remained in order. I called on some of the men to help me find where the other vehicles were before it grew dark. They had all been brought here on transporters and had parked at various points at the edge of the forest. After trying to find the transporters, we contacted all the company's drivers and began to remove the vehicles from their carriers. Only an officer is permitted to unload the vehicle from its carrier, so Achikam and I took over and then told the drivers to take them to the company meeting point. In the dark, we used flashlights and prearranged signals to direct them. Once we reached the meeting point, we arranged them in a column, Karabaki providing us with a number for each vehicle corresponding to the number plate. We checked that everything was in order.

"What about the ammunition for the machine gun?" asked Avshalom.

"We haven't any at present but Karabaki is arranging it. Is there anything else missing?" I asked.

"No, everything's fine. I let the men add some snacks – they get fed up with field rations, so I let them add some cookies and drinks. Don't worry – there are some for your men too. They even asked me what drinks you prefer."

I smiled. "You can rely on them!" I said, half to Avshalom and half to myself.

At the back of the command jeep was a bundle of maps and intelligence material. Karabaki spread them out on the hood, and the company officers crowded together to look at them, holding them down against the wind. "What's happened to the quality of the aerial photos?" asked Achikam.

"They're in black and white?" cried Gete in disappointment. "In Gaza, it was easy to read them because everything was in color."

A tank officer who happened to be passing called out, "Do you know when those maps were made? They look to me as if they're from the 1948 War of Independence, or at the very best from the First Lebanon War of 1982."

I looked at the corner of the aerial photographs and saw that they were dated sometime in 2002. Who knew how many changes had occurred in recent years? They were old and had not been updated. In Gaza, we had become accustomed to the high quality of such aids and were surprised that those for Lebanon were so poor.

Once again, not all our men participated in the operation, to the disappointment of those who remained behind in Israel. Beyond the usual disappointment was also a feeling among the soldiers left behind that they would miss out on a historical event by not setting foot on Lebanese soil and participating in the battle. Some of the soldiers were trying to figure out why their assignments had been changed. The reason was operational. The overall purpose had changed, and as a result changes occurred in assigning the soldiers.

They grumbled, "They're always making changes. It's time they reached a decision."

"The senior officers are always altering the company's mission. We're a company, not a small squad."

An officer tried to explain to them that just as a platoon commander might change one soldier for another or alter the tasks of the various squads, so a division commander can alter the tasks assigned to companies as well as the battalion's missions.

The operation planned for Monday was moved up a day, so that Operation Steel Web began on Sunday night, July 23, at the town of Bint Jbeil. In fact, it was Operation Steel Web Two, the second of two operations in a series of ground attacks in South Lebanon. The name was derived from a well-known speech by Nasrallah, the head of Hezbollah, delivered shortly after Israel's hasty withdrawal from Lebanon in 2000. He had compared Israel's army to a spider's web. He claimed that Israel's army may look strong from the outside, but that it could be conquered and destroyed as easily as a cobweb. Israel may be portrayed as a great military power with technological superiority, but its society cannot stand up to terrorist attacks and shelling. Its society, tired of war, has no strength or resilience to fight gory battles and absorb casualties, he told his audience. In the face of these statements, it was decided to call the operation "Steel Web," indicating that our society, in fact, possessed the strength and power of steel. The operation was part of the overall campaign named "Operation Fair Price," but the name was changed later to "Operation About-Turn," and it finally crystallized as "The Second Lebanon War." At the time, the name did not bother us; nobody realized we were going to war.

Our company was now incorporated into the Fifty-Second Armored Battalion, attached to the Golani Brigade, whose mission was to attack the town of Bint Jbeil. The Brigade entered Bint Jbeil on foot, crossing the fence by the hidden entrance that had been breached near the orchard of Avivim. Egoz entered first, the Fifty-First Battalion next, and then the Reconnaissance Battalion of the Golani Brigade. Bint Jbeil was about three-and-a-half kilometers from the border, a town consisting of about twelve thousand houses. It had a normal population of over thirty thousand, mostly Shi'ites, but most residents had left their homes when fighting broke out in the area. According to Intelligence, scores of Hezbollah terrorists had barricaded themselves in the town, building bunkers and launching pads there. For that reason, it had been nicknamed "The Ḥezbollah Capital."

We boarded our vehicle, but were held up at the entry point till Monday morning because of the missing ammunition. We bedded down for the night around the vehicle, with only a few sleeping bags and, of course, no beds. I stayed up, studying once again the map and intelligence aids, reading them by the dim light inside the vehicle. I heard voices from the other vehicles:

"Lebanon! Sounds like a movie."

"Some movie! We probably won't do a thing. Didn't you hear what Asael said – we'll only be going in a short way. Nothing's going to happen."

"What's all this about a Steel Web? Nasrallah's probably hiding in one of the bunkers with cobwebs all around. Perhaps that's what he was talking about."

Soon, the voices died down, replaced by the sound of people sleeping, itself drowned by the sound of engines and distant explosions.

Then Colonel Gvaram Haglili, the head of Safety and Quality Control, suddenly appeared, yelling, "Men, where are your officers? How can you sleep like this? Do you want to be injured before you go into battle?" He was quite right, there was a real danger. There were vehicles close by and the men could – Heaven forbid! – have been run over. We took up safer positions for sleep, marking the area with stick lights.

I lay on the ground, gazing at the brightly shining stars and trying to distinguish the constellations. I used to love watching them when on field trips. How hard it had been to teach the men during field exercises to identify the North Star, the Big Dipper, and other aids to navigation. Nowadays, we have compasses, so that a knowledge of the stars is less necessary.

In the early hours of Monday morning, the boxes of ammunition arrived. We loaded them, and set out in a column toward the border. One soldier read aloud *Tefillat HaDerekh*, followed by the Prayer Before Going into Battle:

O Lord of Hosts, God of Israel, who is enthroned upon the *keruvim*, You commanded us in Your Torah as follows: "Hear O Israel! Today you are going to war against your enemies. Let not your hearts faint, fear not, and do not tremble, nor be terrified because of them; for the Lord your God is He that goes with you, to fight for you against your enemies, to save you. And now, lo, your enemies make a tumult: and those who hate you have lifted up the head." We beg of You, be with the soldiers of the army of Israel, the emissaries of Your people, who are entering battle today to combat their enemies. Strengthen them and give them courage. Take hold of shield and buckler. Arise for our help, and redeem us for the sake of Your steadfast love. Save us, God, we pray You: we pray You, God, prosper us. Give us help against the foe: for vain is the help of man. Through God we shall do valiantly: for it is He who will tread down our enemies.

We reached the border. Gal informed the company over the communications system that we were about to cross. The men were both excited and anxious. It was difficult to absorb that we too were about to participate in the battle.

Lebanon – how many tales we had heard about it! – the battle lines, the outposts, the heroism of the fighters, but also what was termed the "Lebanese mud," the killed and wounded, as well as the political wrangling and the "Four Mothers" movement.

From the information that had been given to me on the previous day, I knew that we were supposed to enter about five hundred meters beyond the border fence in the direction of Maroun A-Ras, and to wait for orders, functioning as a brigade reserve unit. The vehicle of Second Platoon Commander, Achikam Halpern, had broken down inside Israeli territory and was waiting for repair. We had just settled into position when we were alerted that two tanks had been hit.

"Bungalow Three, this is Kodkod. Move over! Move over! Make way for the tanks behind you!"

Two tanks sped downhill from the fence toward us. I shouted to the driver on our radio: "Igor, pull to the left!" The vehicle struggled uphill against the mud. With the engine roaring and the vehicle shooting up a cloud of dust and stones, it managed to pull off the path. The tanks passed by us, leaving behind a trail of dust. I switched back the radio to the battalion frequency and could hear shouting:

"The tank's on fire! The tank's on fire!"

"Open up the flaps, get them out!"

"Where's Kodkod? Give me Kodkod!"

"This is Kodkod on his way to you."

We heard snatches of conversation. Everyone was speaking at once, nothing could be distinguished. We gathered that the armored battalion commander had been wounded. I told my men to be ready for action. As we had only just entered Lebanon, they were still wearing their flak jackets and helmets.

They grabbed their weapons, ready for action. Karabaki directed me in code over the radio: "Follow north on the map from our position. That's the hill we are supposed to capture." Anxiously, I followed his directions on the map and realized that the plan was to capture Jbeil Kaḥil. In the few minutes left to me, I examined the map again. Then came the order: "Move!" We followed in the tanks' tracks which indicated, to our relief, that the path was clear of mines. I concentrated on the route, directing the driver while the gunner scanned the territory through his periscope.

The tanks had been hit while attempting to rescue some soldiers from Bint Jbeil, who had been wounded by fire coming from the Egoz and Orev Units as well as from the Air Force. The Egoz Unit had just rescued the team commander, Ariel Gino, who had been hit by sniper fire from our forces, when he was then bitten by an attack dog from the Oketz Unit. Gino was a close friend of mine from the officers' course where we had been cadets in the same team, but it was only a few days later that I heard of his injury. During the process of rescuing Gino, the Egoz Unit had come under fire from the Golani's Orev Anti-Tank Unit. The brigade ordered the Air Force to attack the house occupied by the Orev Unit. Its deputy company commander, Gidon Goldenberg, was seriously wounded by the missile they fired, as were a number of other men. At that time I did not know Gidon, but we came to know each other later in the hospital during our lengthy periods of rehabilitation. The Fifty-Second Battalion from the 401ˢᵗ Brigade of the Armored Corps was attached to the Golani Brigade to assist in the rescue. The first tank hit had been under the command of Lieutenant Lotan Slavin; on his way back from Bint Jbeil, laden with the wounded, his tank had been hit by a missile and Lotan killed on the spot. The commander of the Fifty-Second Battalion, Lt. Col. Guy Kabili, tried to reach the damaged tank to assist, but his tank hit a mine. Kobi Smilag was killed, Kabili, the battalion commander, was wounded in the arm and two other crew members injured. Some of the wounded were rescued by a tank near the scene, and the other soldiers trapped in the tank were rescued by a company of engineers.

Major Eli Michelson, deputy commander of the Fifty-Second Battalion, was put in charge of the rescue mission, which took place under heavy covering fire, as well as fire from Ḥezbollah's forces. Dr. Marina Kaminsky of the Fifty-Second Battalion, the only female doctor to enter Lebanon during the war, dealt with the wounded. Maru Gete, the First Platoon commander, went in seated on the rear platform of a tank in order to remove the body of the dead officer. The scene was horrifying: blood smeared on the walls, the smell of burnt flesh, and, hardest of all, the sight of the deceased's body. Maru told me later that the scene left its mark on his troops, and it was difficult to rouse them to further action. He decided that the soldiers who had participated in the evacuation should continue to function in Lebanon in order to help them overcome the trauma they had experienced.

My platoon was sent with another unit to clear out Jbeil Kaḥil, a hill near Maroun A-Ras overlooking the town of Bint Jbeil and the villages Aitaroun and Ainata. It was believed that the anti-tank missiles had been fired from this hill. We reached the ridge between Jbeil-Al-Caucasus on which Maroun A-Ras is located, and Jbeil Kaḥil. On the ridge was the "Pagoda," a wide two-story building visible above the line of the hill. Deserted, it served as an advanced command post and dwelling for forces on alert, its red roof-tiles making it visible from afar. Surrounded by a wall, the southern part was covered in scaffolding, indicating that it had been in the process of being rebuilt or repaired. When we reached it, it was occupied by the Egoz Unit. Nearby, there was a makeshift parking lot for army vehicles and from there we left on foot in order to capture the hill.

In the past, we had frequently taken part in exercises attacking an open target, and various commands from those training sessions ran through my head: "We are under attack, take cover and return fire!" "Platoon! we're under attack two hundred meters ahead, there's a Syrian unit entrenched there. Advance by stages!" "Prepare to charge!" "Prepare to fire – fire! Charge!" It seemed that our training was disconnected from reality. Fighting in the open might be relevant for battle but we were engaged in urban warfare. Now was the time to translate our training into action.

I led the platoon up the hill. Gal, the company commander, was in charge, and he was advancing slightly behind our platoon. We started climbing the hill, encountering rough terrain covered with thistles. Small fires were burning higher up the hill, probably caused by falling shells. The fire licked the dry thistles, but despite the wind, did not spread toward us. We changed direction to avoid its spiraling smoke. On surveying the territory and identifying some suspicious objects, we opened fire on them, while Yigal and Benizri, the machine gunners, raked them. Then we halted behind a depression in the ground, hesitant to expose ourselves by raising our heads. Who knew whether there were still terrorists there? No doubt they had already identified us as we climbed up, shooting as we went. The tanks' observation turrets helped us in surveillance. Karabaki requested assistance from the tankers in combing the area above, and only when they reported that there was no sign of the enemy did we advance toward the summit. At the same time the gunner equipped with a special grenade-shooter fired at a suspicious target near one of the trees. Where could they be hidden? We searched the area and shot at targets. Perhaps they had withdrawn to the village? Maybe they had never fired from this hill.

After determining that there was no anti-tank unit there, we took up daytime positions overlooking Aitaroun, Bint Jbeil, and Ainata. Taking up daytime positions in such an area was dangerous, as it was difficult to take cover in the rocky terrain, especially in light of our haste. Lots of pamphlets that had been dropped by the Air Force on the villages of South Lebanon had been scattered by the wind onto the hillside. I picked up one of them. "They look like advertisements," said Uri, the squad commander. Yigal, who could read Arabic, translated the text:

> To the people of Lebanon:
>
> Following the unbridled terrorism being conducted by Hezbollah, actions that undermine efforts to build a better future for Lebanon, the IDF has entered Lebanon for as long as proves necessary to protect the citizens of Israel. As we wish to avoid injury to innocent civilians, you are advised to avoid areas in which Hezbollah is active. Remember that continued terrorism against Israel is a two-edged sword, threatening both you and Lebanon at large.
>
> The State of Israel

It was part of a propaganda campaign against Hezbollah. The obvious aim of the leaflets was to keep innocent civilians away from terrorist centers, but I tried to think how I would react if I were a resident of Lebanon and read a leaflet like that. Would I be angry with Israel? Or perhaps with Hezbollah? Anyway, I thought I would try to keep my family away from the battle areas. Indeed, in all the villages we passed through during the battle, we saw scarcely any civilians. Most had probably moved north to the Litani River, far from the fighting.

In the evening, we received permission to leave the ambush point, and a unit from Egoz came to relieve us. The next day, Achikam, the commander of the Second Platoon who had joined us after his vehicle was repaired, took over from them. For the next few days we set up rotations on Jbeil Kahil, with the reservists from the Golani Reconnaissance Unit joining in. Every rota began with a session in which the commander of the unit updated everyone on the location of the ambush, established a common set of surveillance terms, and defined the rules for opening fire and for responding to other possible eventualities. After about half an hour, during which everyone remained awake, there began the sleep rosters, ensuring that there was always a section of the unit on the alert. The roster was based on what we called "Brass Pairs," a system in which two soldiers were assigned as a pair, with one of them always awake.

The view from the hilltop was breathtaking: green hills as in Galilee, but more virgin, as there was little human habitation and, where there was, it blended into the landscape. Throughout our stay there, we could see constant shelling by Israeli artillery, aided by the Air Force. We grew used to the massive shelling and the explosions. Above us flew Israeli planes and helicopters sending out heat-attracting anti-missile flares. We learned in time to identify the artillery shells zooming over our heads, to see where they landed and to watch them explode after a few moments. In daytime, we could see the smoke rising from the place of the explosion, and at night the flash of light. Running through my head was the verse from the Book of Exodus: "The pillar of cloud will not move from My nation by day nor the pillar of fire by night." The numerous shellings provided us with a protective curtain of smoke. Whenever we identified Katyusha counter-shelling, we reported the fact, to help the artillery pinpoint the location of the launch and the terrorists activating it.

The unit that had been relieved from the ambush point stayed in the armored vehicles' parking lot, prepared for perimeter defense. Apart from our own vehicles, there were tanks of the Fifty-Second Battalion and bulldozers belonging to the Engineering Corps. Both the Pagoda and the parking lot served as points for deployment and for the replacement of equipment. At night, a force from the Third Rifles led by battalion deputy commander Klein, distributed intelligence material in the form of computer disks, together with radio equipment discovered in the process of searching the buildings and the bodies of dead terrorists.

Lieutenant Colonel Tzachi Segev, the former commander of the Fifty-Second Battalion, was appointed to replace the wounded Kabili as battalion commander. At a meeting with Segev, we arranged the security zones in the parking lot. It was difficult to keep soldiers awake while looking through the vehicle's periscopes, but to keep them inside was preferable to exposing them to falling shrapnel. From time to time, there were explosions close to us, from mortar shells fired at us, or from IDF artillery fire that came a little too close. The drill adopted was simple: to keep all the men inside the vehicles wearing protective equipment including flak jackets and helmets, and then to close up the vehicles.

The soldiers tried to pass the time inside. When they grew tired of playing games, they began imitating officers and soldiers in the company. I tried to concentrate on reading the map, but it was impossible to ignore the impersonations, so I tried to hide my smile behind the large map. Suddenly, the lights went out. I checked the control panel's lights, worried that the batteries had run down, but found that a cell phone charger had been plugged into the vehicle's battery outlet; Sharon had discovered a creative solution for charging their phone batteries. I started up the vehicle and, to the disappointment of the men, forbade any tinkering with the vehicle's batteries.

Our lengthy stay inside the vehicle created a special closeness among us as, during that period, we did everything together: eating, sleeping, talking, laughing, and preparing for battle. The proximity removed the barriers that sometimes arise between an officer and his men. I felt more free in talking with them, and they too felt freer and more open with me. They told me of amusing incidents that had occurred during training, some known to me but some not. They, on their part, were interested in learning what considerations lay behind certain decisions, from job assignments to the punishments meted out to soldiers. I told them how I frequently canceled punishment when there was a reasonable doubt, preferring to let a soldier go unpunished rather than to punish one undeservedly. I told them about my personal life, and especially the jobs I had had in the army, such as how I had served as radio operator for the platoon commander, which was the reason I was especially strict about communications during drills and training. I knew the problems but I had also learned from them. I enjoyed the open atmosphere that had been created; we felt more united and hence more reliant on each other.

During our stay in the area, a team of engineers was dispatched to attempt to rescue the two damaged tanks of the Fifty-Second

Battalion, and was attacked by terrorists who hurtled out of the dark in jeeps. The engineer soldiers responded by launching a ground missile at the terrorists. The explosion ended the incident with no casualties to our forces and an unknown number of casualties among the terrorists. The missile actually hit the jeeps, so that nothing was left to determine whether any of the terrorists had managed to escape. It was a very original use of a device intended to clear roads of mines, not for direct combat with the enemy.

In the parking lot, piles of garbage had accumulated and trash was scattered around. The lot did not look as orderly as an IDF site should. Gal took up the matter with me and insisted that we clean up the area around our vehicles. I was hesitant about sending the soldiers out of the vehicle to collect the garbage and clean the area. In principle, the IDF is particular about garbage for two main reasons. One is environmental, although admittedly that principle is more applicable when we are training in Israel and try to keep the country clean. Yet we also try to avoid harming nature in enemy country. The second reason is operational, since leaving trash exposes a position even after forces have exited the area, leaving signs that could help the enemy follow our tracks. That argument holds particularly true for ambushes and camouflaged positions. However, it was much less valid for our situation, where sending soldiers to clean up meant taking them out of their armored vehicles and exposing them to danger. They did often leave their vehicles for operational reasons, but it seemed unjustified to endanger them for reasons of hygiene. We decided, therefore, that those soldiers who had to leave their vehicles for operational reasons should, while wearing their flak jackets and helmets, spend a few extra minutes piling the large garbage bags in one central place. We also gave orders that, in future, garbage should be disposed of more effectively.

On Tuesday afternoon, an order came to prepare to exit Bint Jbeil and return to Israel, but the order was changed that evening and it was decided that we should stay in Lebanon another twenty-four hours. Later, we were given a new mission: to go into Bint Jbeil and bring back some terrorist corpses (probably required for exchange purposes), and to bring supplies to the brigade forces located there. We received a large number of packages, which included our own supplies.

Apart from food, water, and ammunition, we were given a folder containing "Notes on Fighting in Lebanon" issued by the Intelligence Department of the Ground Forces Command. In this brief booklet were gathered lessons that had been learned from recent engagements in Lebanon by the Maglan and Egoz Units, with emphasis on the difference between fighting there and in Gaza or Judea and Samaria.

I walked over to Gal's vehicle to obtain details about the route we would take. We began to plan the route and the units to be employed, but the mission was held up because of intelligence that there were terrorists in the area.

It was a very dark night with no moon – the first of the month of Av, in which we mourn the Destruction of both Temples – hence the saying: "When Av arrives, joy is reduced." The rabbis also recommended that, if anyone has a court case with a non-Jew he should avoid Av, the month of calamities.

On Wednesday, July 26, we were in the parking lot on the ridge between Jbeil-Al-Caucasus and Jbeil Kaḥil when we received an order to advance more deeply into the center of the town, into the "Black Polygon" (the area around the kasbah marked on the maps in black), but not to enter the kasbah itself. We were also ordered to move our men to different buildings, as it was suspected that those we were occupying had been identified by the Ḥezbollah. In the early hours, we moved our troops, the Fifty-First Battalion, a few hundred meters to different buildings in Bint Jbeil.

At 5:00 a.m., the Third Rifles were involved in a long and bloody battle. We did not know specifics, but heard explosions, the sound of helicopters, and disturbing reports on the radio, later confirmed, indicating that something serious was occurring. A unit that was in an ambush position in Jbeil Kaḥil could see the area of the fighting, the smoke from the explosions, and helicopters arriving one after the other, but orders came not to move in that direction until the situation had become clearer. We waited anxiously, ready to advance to their assistance. During the day, rumors were rife, mostly unofficial, that there had been a high number of fatalities and that the chain of command had suffered a serious blow. It was only later that we learned the details.

From those involved, we eventually discovered what had happened that day. The Third Rifles had been moving a few hundred meters northwest to the buildings assigned to them. The Lead Platoon under Amichai Merchavia was supposed to enter the building on the east side. The platoon entered the courtyard together with the unit under Roi Klein, the deputy battalion commander, and Alex Shwartsman, the deputy company commander. They attempted to break the lock of the iron gate blocking access to the service room that led, in turn, to the main room of the building. After attempts to break it with a hydraulic device failed, Klein ordered Evyatar Dahan to fire two grenades at the lock, and he also fired at it with his own weapon, but again, to no avail. As the unit had no door-breaking device, Alex went off to obtain an explosive brick from a nearby unit. Throughout the incident, the men remained crouched next to the courtyard wall. Evyatar Cohen ("Gingy"), the unit machine gunner, scanning the area with his night goggles suddenly saw a figure a short distance beyond the wall wearing a uniform but no helmet, and armed with a Kalashnikov rifle. Many of the terrorists wore IDF uniforms and carried Israeli weapons to make it difficult to distinguish them from our soldiers. Surprised to see him, Gingy opened fire. Amichai suspected it might be an Israeli but Gingy, describing what he had seen, claimed he was certain it was a terrorist.

Then fire opened up from other directions and a battle began that lasted over ten hours. Amichai reported over the company radio: "We've been attacked from the rear by a terrorist wearing no helmet." There were short exchanges of fire between the terrorists hiding behind the wall and the Lead Platoon on the other side, taking cover there behind the olive trees in the courtyard. Klein threw a grenade over the wall and ordered the men to fire and lob grenades. One of the grenades thrown by them hit an iron bar projecting from the wall and rolled back near the fighters. Evyatar Dahan noticed it, kicked it away, and it exploded without causing any casualties.

During the exchange of fire, Klein shouted, "We are being attacked from the east! Lie down, return fire, and we'll carry out a flanking maneuver!" The soldiers called back acknowledging the order. Klein reported over the radio: "Klein speaking – we've been attacked from the rear!" The advance group under Amichai climbed ahead into the upper olive grove and moved against the terrorists in a right-flanking movement. He reported over the radio, and then called to his men: "Terrorists ahead – storm them!" They rushed forward, but were blocked by another wall encircling that grove. The terrorists hiding there rained down bullets and grenades on the unit caught in the upper grove. Amichai, wounded at the beginning of the attack by two bullets in his right hand, continued the charge toward the wall, but was critically wounded by a grenade exploding nearby. He continued to report over the radio in a voice growing ever weaker. Gingy was also wounded by that grenade, in the shoulder, and Evyatar Dahan was hit by a bullet, also in his shoulder. Ohad Klauzner, the sharpshooter of the advance unit, stopped to treat Evyatar. Shimon Dahan, the platoon sergeant, who was behind them, joined the fighting, together with seven additional soldiers. Immediately after, as he was leading his men to the wall, he was critically wounded by a grenade and later died of his wounds. The others returned fire and treated the wounded.

Klein, having heard Amichai's report over the radio, advanced together with his radio operator, Yohai Reani, to help with the wounded. Alex stopped them before they entered the upper grove so that he could activate the explosive brick. After the explosion had opened up entry to the building, Klein and Yohai advanced toward the wounded who were lying near the wall in the upper grove. Klein, together with Yohai and Evyatar Turgeman, the squad commander, helped load Amichai onto a stretcher and Shimon Adega and Assaf Namer treated his wounds. Just before that, Shiran Amsili had passed along an empty stretcher that Shimon Adega had been carrying on his back. Assaf Namer stood up, shooting over the wall, until he was hit by two bullets in the head and killed instantly.

Another grenade exploded at Roi Klein's feet. According to reports, Roi spotted the grenade thrown at the soldiers, and sacrificed himself to save his soldiers by lying on it. He was critically wounded and tried to report on the radio, "This is Klein dying, Klein dying," having recognized the seriousness of his condition. Shortly after, he recited the prayer, "Hear O Israel…" and then, hit by another grenade,

Roi Klein returned his soul to his Creator. His radio operator, Yohai, was also wounded by grenade shrapnel, as were many others. Before Roi died, Evyatar Turgeman, the squad commander of the advance unit, tried, together with Shimon Adega, to drag him to the wall. Klein shouted to them that they should take Merchavia instead. While they were lifting the stretcher, another grenade exploded near them. Shimon Adega was critically wounded in the legs and later died of his wounds, after being taken to the unit's building. Evyatar Turgeman was injured in the hand.

Alex finished breaking into the building, heard the reports on the radio, and with his contact, Idan Cohen, joined those in the upper olive grove to assist them. Both were wounded in the lower limbs, Idan severely. Alex Shwartsman encouraged him: "Don't worry, we'll get out of here." Later, Idan, evacuated to the department's building, despite his severe injuries and intolerable pain, encouraged the wounded around him; but he eventually died of his wounds. Alex, leaning against an olive tree, kept calling to the soldiers to rescue Merchavia, and despite his injury, kept in touch with Alon Hakima, the company commander and Asor, the battalion commander. He described the scene of the battle: "We have numerous casualties, the terrorists are lobbing grenades over the wall. Outflank them!"

Alon, the company commander, joined the battle area under Alex's direction, accompanied by Itamar Katz, a past company commander, Maoz, the patrol platoon commander, and other fighters. While they were performing an outflanking maneuver, they ran into fire from the northern building. The soldiers returned fire and Maoz shot a LAW rocket at the building that silenced the source of fire. As the force was blocked by a high wall encircling the building, Alon altered their line of approach, reaching the rear of the upper olive grove where the wounded were lying. The unit threw grenades, wounding the terrorists on the other side of the wall. Alon placed Shiran Amsili, the machine gunner, close by to block any other terrorists attempting to approach. Katz treated Klein, who handed over to him the "Rose of Sharon" code radio. Alon Hakima was seriously wounded by fire while attempting to rescue Gingy, and Maoz was hit in the head. Yoni Roth, the squad commander of the patrol unit, and Sharabi began a left-flanking movement, but both were hit, and managed to evacuate themselves to the rear.

Another force from the Patrol Platoon reached the upper plantation, an area exposed to withering fire. Avichay Yaakov, a squad commander in the company, led the rescue during the battle after his sergeant, Degen, had been wounded. They kept entering and exiting with the wounded. After an hour and a half, Ohad Klauzner was mortally wounded by sniper fire in the course of the rescue. Alex Shwartsman refused to be moved, insisting that the other wounded be evacuated first. At the end of the operation, while Avichay was dragging Alex along by his right leg and Alex assisted with his left, Alex was hit in the neck and chest by sniper fire, dying in Avichay's arms.

Avichay contacted the battalion commander by radio, reporting on the number of dead and the fact that they were still being fired on. Upon being told to fire back, he reported that they had run out of ammunition. Eventually, he and Yisrael Ben-Lulu collected ammunition from the pouches of those killed. Shiran, the machine gunner, looking over the wall, saw three terrorists approaching. He squeezed the trigger, hitting them with the last bullets in his magazine.

The area was being shot at from five directions, so that the number of casualties was high. Eleven out of twelve fighters in the advance unit entering the olive grove had been wounded, and more than two-thirds of all those who fought there. Rescuing them was especially difficult. The drones that constantly accompany brigade forces were able to focus their cameras on the battlefield, but those interpreting the photos were unable to distinguish with any certainty between our forces and those of the enemy. For that, and for certain other reasons, they were unable to make any real-time contribution.

As a result of the severe damage to the force's chain of command (the deputy battalion commander, the company commander, the deputy company commander, two platoon commanders, and two sergeants), Itamar Katz took over. He placed covering forces by the wall and on the second floor of the building that had been broken into earlier by Alex. Katz told Shuvi, the commander of the saboteur platoon, to conduct a deep right-flanking movement but it came under fire and was ordered to withdraw. During the fighting, intelligence was received that terrorists intended to abduct soldiers. A security unit under the command of Yoni Zano, the sergeant of the saboteur platoon, remained outside the building to prevent the possibility of abduction. Katz placed a covering unit commanded by Moshe Nahum in the building. Sasha, the sharpshooter, who took up a covering position at the entrance to the building, was fired on but continued to shoot, hitting terrorists. Katz ordered the company medic to set up a collection point for the wounded in the main room of the building, where casualties were brought in, divided according to their degrees of injury into severe, medium, and light, and where they received medical treatment.

While Riflemen Company C was engaged in the fighting, other companies were also fighting terrorists in an attempt to isolate the area of the fighting and help provide cover. Yisrael Friedler, company commander of Riflemen Company A, was hit by a sniper's bullet but continued to fight and lead the company. Brigade headquarters reported to Asor, the battalion commander, that they had identified armed men near a mosque. The battalion commander made sure that they were not our troops and gave orders to fire at them. They were killed by air fire.

Yoni Chetboun, the operations officer of the Fifty-First Battalion, organized a squad of soldiers from Company A, and went to help. On their way, they were shot at, and one of the men, wounded in the leg, was evacuated to the building, accompanied by a sergeant. In one grove, they discovered a launching pad. Yoni informed the battalion commander so that it could be destroyed later. The force under Yoni joined up with Company C under Katz, a friend of his, and the two embraced when they met. Together they tried to identify the area with the aid of the intelligence maps in order to direct Air Force fire. However, the maps were out-of-date, and some of the houses did not appear in them, so that the Air Force was afraid the missiles might hit our forces, both because of the close range and because of the multiple sources of fire. But they did assign two helicopters to the unit. Yoni marked by means of a smoke bomb the building that did not appear on the map, and directed the helicopters to the sources of fire. Heavy fire had been directed from several buildings, including the mosque. Attack helicopters fired missiles accurately at the source of fire, and the shooting from there died down. Under cover of the helicopters, the bodies of the fallen soldiers were removed from the courtyard into the building.

The exchange of fire continued for a long time, during which soldiers hit more terrorists and rescued the last victims, evacuating them from the area of operations. The men of Riflemen Company A and the Auxiliary Company, who were assisting, saw terrorists fleeing from the heavy fire provided by Company C, and hit them.

Itamar Katz ordered a medic to list the condition of all members of the company. It was scribbled in blue pen on a triangular bandage, Katz using it to take command of the situation. He contacted Asor, the battalion commander, and read him the list of the fallen.

By about eleven o'clock, all the wounded had been evacuated by stages to the helipad. They were taken by the Engineers and Demolition Unit, accompanied by two medics, to the building occupied by Riflemen A. They were moved to the meeting point with the Golani Reconnaissance Unit, and from there to the makeshift helicopter pad. The evacuation took place under fire, in intense heat, and through difficult terrain. Five Black Hawk helicopters belonging to Rescue Unit 669 landed briefly. They took turns landing, loading the wounded – more than twenty in number – and evacuating them to Rambam Hospital in Israel. After the evacuation, information was received from Intelligence of another attack by Hezbollah, so the battalion commander decided to postpone the evacuation of the bodies, which were kept in a building near the battle area for that night.

The battle was over, and we had achieved superiority. Dozens of terrorists belonging to Hezbollah's special force had been killed and the remainder had fled, but the results on our side were particularly painful: eight dead and dozens wounded. These are the names of the members of the Fifty-First Battalion killed in Bint Jbeil:

Major Roi Klein from Eli, Captain Alex Shwartsman from Acre, Lieutenant Amichai Merchavia from Eli, Staff Sergeant Idan Cohen from Jaffa, Staff Sergeant Shimon Dahan from Ashdod, Staff

Sergeant Ohad Klauzner from Beit Ḥoron, Sergeant Shimon Adega from Kiryat Gat, and Sergeant Assaf Namer from Sydney, Australia.

As mentioned, we were only a few hundred yards from the incident, yet knew no details of the battle. We had not received permission to enter Bint Jbeil to help in the rescue, and had to wait anxiously in our vehicle. After Gal told me that Roi Klein, the deputy commander of the Fifty-First Battalion had been killed, I dared to ask how Amichai Merchavia was. I had heard that he was seriously hurt and now there was a rumor that he was dead. I received no clear answer, and because it was hard to grasp the possibility of his being dead, I continued to hope he was alive.

A strained silence prevailed after the battle. I decided to send a text message reassuring my parents. I did not mention that a fierce battle had taken place that morning and that we had suffered many battalion casualties, but I wrote that we had completed our mission and were waiting for the next task. I was afraid that my parents would hear disturbing reports from the media and would be unable to verify the situation. It later turned out that my parents had been saved considerable worry. Earlier that day, my father had telephoned to comfort his childhood friend, Moshe Muskal, the father of Refanael who had fallen in Egoz in the fighting at Maroun A-Ras. At that moment, Brigadier General Eli Reiter, the commander of the Thirty-Sixth Division, happened to be in Muskal's home. He had received reports of the battle at Bint Jbeil and knew that the Fifty-First Battalion had suffered many casualties, including several officers. Moshe Muskal spoke with my father and learned from him that I was serving as a platoon commander in the Fifty-First Battalion, but my father had not yet heard of the battle. Moshe decided not to tell my father the news he had heard from Reiter but, as he later admitted, while my father was comforting him, it crossed his mind that he might have to comfort my father.

That night, we went out to set another ambush. I tried to concentrate on the task, but my mind kept wandering. Memories of past days spent with Amichai kept surfacing in my mind. Was it right to think about it? Maybe Amichai was still alive, fighting for his life in the hospital? Maybe I should think only of the ambush and not let other thoughts distract me? I stared into the dark and checked that the men were all alert. A few hours later, I was informed on the company radio that we had been assigned a new mission.

We ended the ambush and Egoz came to replace us. During the night, a force of the Golani Reconnaissance Battalion evacuated the bodies of those who had fallen to a meeting point south of Bint Jbeil. Soldiers of the Twelfth Battalion arrived there with the battalion's supply portfolios that had been taken from us at the Pagoda. Tamir Yadai, the commander of the Golani Brigade, and Roi Levy, the operations officer of the Golani, joined us for the mission, together with two officers attached to the battalion. Major Shuki Ribak was appointed Deputy Battalion Commander, in place of the late Roi Klein, and Major Udi Ben-Hamo took over from Yisrael Friedler, the wounded company commander of Riflemen A.

Soldiers from the Twelfth Battalion brought the stretchers to our location. With them came Friedler, the wounded company commander, together with a soldier from Riflemen C, Yosef Abutbul, who had been lightly wounded in his leg. Tamir, the brigade commander, chatted with Yosef. Only later did we learn that the latter, who had returned to fight with his company, was killed in an operational accident, run over by a tank during an ambush in Lebanon, two-and-a-half weeks later.

Our mission was to lead the funeral cortege back across the border. I gathered the men and, in a few words, explained the solemnity of our responsibility and the importance of the mission. Bringing bodies back to be buried in Israel is a sacred task, an indispensable moral duty owed to those who gave their lives as martyrs. No one needed to be forced to participate in the cortege.

We drove up to the meeting point, the Pagoda, where I met up with Tamir. His expression said it all. On the ground lay eight stretchers, each covered with a blanket, on which lay our friends from the battalion. It was a terrible scene. One soldier sat next to them, reciting Psalms in memory of the fallen. Murmuring the prayers with him, we carefully placed two stretchers in each vehicle.

I lifted one, with the assistance of a soldier. After a few paces, I told him to put it down as it needed straightening. I undid the knots, and lifted the body by the head. To my horror, I found that I was holding the head of Amichai Merchavia. My heart seemed to stop.

I had learned in the most dramatic way that Amichai was no more. He had been a close friend from our earliest days in the army. We were together in the same platoon, we were in the squad commanders' course together, and we continued to remain in close contact during officers' training and while serving as officers in the battalion. We had also spent many hours studying Jewish subjects together, and had enjoyed many heart-to-heart talks.

There are moments when one knows that one's life has changed irrevocably, that things will never be the same again. But it is not always possible to identify the moment. How can one describe one's feeling on confronting the dead? It is indescribable. I had not yet experienced the full shock, but I knew that a chasm had opened before me, an irreparable void.

What makes a single moment produce such change in oneself or in one's friend? Heaven alone has the answers. I had known that Lebanon would be dangerous, that there would be casualties. I had known that some of the casualties would be comrades of mine, and had heard about the lists of the fallen. Nothing, however, prepared me for this moment, for the task of carrying the fallen members of our battalion. The realization that they were dead, that they would never return, hit me hard. From that moment, I grasped to the full that we were at war.

Despite the emotional shock, we continued our task, although the words I spoke seemed divorced from my inner feelings. "Is the vehicle full?" "Did you put two in each?" More questions and talk, as if ignoring the fact that we were talking of friends from our battalion who had been alive only the day before. After driving about three kilometers, we reached the border of Israel opposite Avivim. Near the cypress trees we met a unit of the military rabbinate, due to take over from us and continue the long journey from Lebanon to the official funeral in Israel. With them was Rabbi Avi Ronski, due soon to be appointed Chief Rabbi of the IDF. He inquired how the soldiers in the battalion were managing and encouraged us to

continue the task. After assisting them in the transfer, we remained
outside the vehicles, waiting while any traces of blood left there by
the dead were removed. We changed our bloodstained uniforms,
handing them over for burial in accordance with Jewish tradition.

All those who had taken part in the mission, both officers and
men, gathered together. Gal sadly reminded us that, painful as our
work had been, we could not forget that the war was not over and
we must continue taking strong action against Ḥezbollah.

I read Psalm 23:

> I will lift up mine eyes unto the hills, whence cometh my
> help? My help cometh from the Lord, who made heaven and
> earth. He will not suffer thy foot to be moved: He that keep-
> eth thee will not slumber. Behold, He that keepeth Israel shall
> neither slumber nor sleep. The Lord is thy keeper: the Lord is
> thy shade upon thy right hand. The sun shall not smite thee
> by day, nor the moon by night. The Lord shall preserve thee
> from all evil: He shall preserve thy soul. The Lord shall pre-
> serve thy going out and thy coming in from this time forth,
> and even for evermore.

After dawn on Thursday, we took our *tefillin* from the vehicle
and prepared for morning prayers. I wound the black leather straps
around my arm, feeling it to be a shield between me and reality.
Then, with the straps, I formed on my hand the sign of the letter
shin, marking the first letter in the divine name. I placed the second
of the *tefillin* on my head and tightened the arm straps. Inside the two
small boxes were parchment scrolls containing four passages from the
Bible, one of them containing the verse, "Thou shalt love the Lord
with all thy heart and with all thy soul and with all thy might." The
Mishna, at the end of Tractate Berakhot, explains that "with all thy
soul" means even at the price of one's life.

As I recited the morning prayers, I felt alone with my Creator, a moment of prayer quite different from any other, certainly
from the kind of hasty prayer offered during battle. The men asked
permission to don *tefillin* and to recite the prayer, "Hear O Israel,

the Lord our God, the Lord is One." Many had not donned *tefillin* since the time of their bar mitzva, but now almost all experienced the urge to do so, perhaps through need of spiritual support in the midst of the confusion and tension.

A number of journalists and photographers were waiting for us at the border. We wanted to be left alone, particularly during the period of transferring the bodies, but the photographers pestered us, constantly taking pictures, many of them shots of us putting on *tefillin* and praying. One photo of me, taken by an Israeli photographer named Yoav Lemmer, appeared on the Internet and somehow reached my family. It accompanied me throughout the rehabilitation process.

We were supplied with food and water by Kaplan, the company sergeant major who always cared for our needs. The soldiers switched on their cell phones and called their parents. I reminded them not to specify place names or details of military units, but I forgot to tell them to reassure their parents. I heard one of the soldiers describing the situation to his mother: "There's non-stop shelling and constant firing – it's a miracle we're still alive. Dangerous? It sure is dangerous. Lebanon's in a different league."

A commander took him aside: "Do you know what your mother's going through? Do you want to give her a nervous break-down? Why scare your parents like that?" A soldier standing nearby joined in and told us what he had said to his mother, adding, "If she knew I were here, she'd come straight to Lebanon and take me home! As it is, she hasn't been able to sleep since she heard there was fighting here."

A number of soldiers asked for permission to attend the funerals. I told them that, unfortunately, there was no such possibility, as we had to return to Lebanon and complete the tasks assigned by the battalion. I added that I too felt a strong desire to attend, but in times of war, operational commitments take precedence.

We returned to Lebanon, but while we were still in the vehicle I talked with the soldiers, for this had been their first exposure to death in battle. Many described how they had felt during the difficult task. I explained to them that although outwardly I had behaved as normal during the evacuation, inwardly it had been a very difficult experience, especially the encounter with Amichai's body. They remarked they had observed a change in my behavior since the moment of that encounter, so I told them a little about Amichai and tried to encourage them for what was to follow. We were tired and worn-out, but it was important to maintain combat efficiency. That afternoon, we traveled twice to the border, ferrying the Reconnaissance Unit of the Seventh Armored Brigade, together with its equipment, from Israel to the Pagoda.

On Friday morning, the bodies of Ḥezbollah terrorists were retrieved for possible future exchange. Achikam and his men took them in their vehicle from the Pagoda to the Israeli border. The bodies were in a state of advanced decay after lying in the street for a few days and the men had to wear masks because of the stench. Despite the awful smell and the horrific appearance of the corpses, some men wanted to see the bodies, to lift the covers and photograph them. They felt anger toward them, but we had to prevent any damage to the corpses. Their physical condition was far worse than those of our comrades that we had evacuated the previous night, but this task was much easier.

Immediately after the evacuation, Gal told me to prepare for another ambush. My platoon began to organize for the operation; however, the men were moving sluggishly. I consulted with Avshalom, the platoon sergeant, who felt that we needed to take action as the men were working reluctantly. I called the men together and, in the short time at our disposal, attempted to address the pain we all felt at the loss of our comrades and our obligation to continue performing our task with full efficiency. Sorrow must not be allowed to weaken our resolve lest, as a result, we cause – Heaven forbid! – further casualties.

We set out for the expected attack in a state of advanced exhaustion. I was afraid that, despite the pairing off of soldiers to allow sleep, the men would be unable to stand up to the pressure and would collapse through fatigue. I was exhausted too, but I could not sleep waiting for the attack. My partner, who was supposed to replace me and stay awake, seemed utterly worn out and I did not want to disturb him, so I stayed up for most of the night. At times, I felt that if I did not wake some of the sleeping soldiers, I would be the only one alert. The landscape before us was unchanged, but it had lost its beauty and now appeared simply as a battlefield. The tall domes had become observation posts, the wadis advance routes, the shrubs and rocks hiding places.

We returned from the ambush shortly before sunset that marked the onset of Shabbat. I debated whether to put on *tefillin*, or try to call home, but was worried that my family might have already welcomed in Shabbat, when phoning is forbidden. I decided to put on *tefillin* despite the late hour, hoping that it was not too late. That problem was familiar to me. Rabbi Haim Sabato describes in his book *Adjusting Sights* how, during the Yom Kippur War, after his tank had been hit and he had to leave it, he returned to the damaged tank in the evening, found his *tefillin*, and put them on despite his friend's protest that the sun had already set. He could see that there was still some daylight, so he went ahead.

Gal informed me that our entire brigade was due to leave Lebanon that night. In an unusual step, he permitted the men who desired to pray to do so together inside the Pagoda. A collection of dusty combat soldiers from the Tank Corps, from Egoz, and from our company recited the Friday night service together. At the conclusion, they pronounced Kiddush, the benediction sanctifying Shabbat, and I was asked to say a few words. I knew that it was not the time to delve into a subject demanding concentration, that something short and to the point would be preferable. I mentioned therefore that in Jewish tradition there were certain things that could only be achieved through suffering, and that one of them was the Land of Israel. That was what we were suffering for at this time. In conclusion, I quoted the words of Maimonides, that those who die in the divine cause deserve the highest merit, and I added that our comrades had indeed died in that way, fighting to defend the Holy Land.

During that Shabbat night, all forces withdrew safely from Lebanon. We were afraid the news that we were returning home might cause complacency and decrease operational alertness, but the withdrawal took place with no problems.

Chapter Six

Condolence Calls

Saturday, July 29, 2006–Sunday, July 30, 2006

The battalion reached the Palm Beach Hotel in Acre on Saturday morning. On the way, after ensuring that the driver knew the route to Acre, I dozed off. I was unsure whether it was permitted to travel like this on Shabbat, but realized that we needed the rest, as well as time to prepare for the next operation; it was therefore justified for us to drive to the hotel as we could not stop near the border. However, would it be permissible to drive anywhere else? As I began to doze off, I decided that when we reached Acre I would consult with Yoni Chetboun, the Operations Officer, and with Amichai Merchavia. Then I jerked awake, as though bitten. The grievous fact hit me again: Amichai was dead. It seems that even after the brain has grasped a fact, it takes time for the heart to accept it.

We reached the hotel and met up with the other companies. Everyone was talking about the battle. Weekend newspapers, with pictures of the fallen framed in black, were passed from hand to hand. The men gathered around Yaniv Asor, the battalion commander, and sat together on the hotel lawn, beside the pool, listening to him: "Israel, an eternal nation, must never fear a lengthy struggle. The Fifty-First Battalion and the Golani Brigade have known worse days and have always been able to recover and find the strength to fulfill our missions. I am proud to command such brave warriors. You have proven under fire that you possess the spirit and the power of Jewish fighters, ready to defend your country. The war is not over and the Fifty-First Battalion will continue the battle on the front line." He then introduced two new officers: "Join our ranks, you veteran foxes of war, Shuki Ribak and Udi Ben-Hamo. You will strengthen the battalion for future fighting. I have visited all the battalion's wounded in hospital and they wish us luck..." Achikam remarked that, throughout his talk, Yaniv had never mentioned the names of the fallen, no doubt to avoid disheartening the men. He preferred to reassure them.

After the talk, we ate a meal on the lawn, a meal that, after a week of field rations and bread, ought to have been a pleasure. But I had lost my sense of taste, and the food seemed bland. Profound sadness made material enjoyment seem meaningless.

We slept at a hostel in Peki'in where we received packages containing toiletries, snacks, underwear and, of course, fresh uniforms. The battalion officers met with the brigade's organizational consultant, a psychologist by profession, who advised us on how to deal with problems liable to arise in our platoons. The consultant explained the significance of maintaining a sense of cohesion; after experiencing a loss, it is essential to strengthen the framework in order to preserve personal and organizational stability.

At the Peki'in hostel we met the other soldiers from our company who had not been with us in Lebanon. Although only a week had passed since we had seen each other, it seemed like an era. The stubble that had grown on our cheeks during that week offered mute testimony that we had matured, even aged. The sense of comradeship between the men who had experienced the terrible events of the past week was not shared by those who had not been there.

I heard voices from the corridor:

"Anyone have any shampoo?"

"Is your towel dry? Can I use it?"

"When do we get our spare uniforms?"

"Will we get leave on Sunday?"

"Asael!" one of the soldiers called. "Is it true we're leaving this evening?"

It felt strange to be dealing once again with routine matters, as if nothing had changed, but such is the power of routine, returning us to normal life.

On Saturday night, I delivered a talk to the men, summarizing the course of the last week's events, from our entry into Lebanon, through the ambushes, and concluding with the period of waiting in our vehicle, then the battle, and the evacuation of the fallen. I told them I was proud of their performance during the week. I thought to myself that there lay the strength of these young fighters. Although one has to deal with problems of motivation and discipline routinely, at the moment of truth the Golani soldiers do not disappoint. They are fighters, they know how to attack, to rescue their comrades under fire, to maintain operational discipline; and the brotherhood of fellow fighters assumes for them a special significance.

To wrap up, I described the very difficult moment I had experienced when evacuating the body of Amichai Merchavia. At this point, I asked the men to share with others their experiences and feelings. Many simply lowered their gaze, but a few did speak up. They discussed the events, but could find no words to describe their feelings. I felt that the conversation could progress no further. At that moment, I had to end, as the buses had arrived. I concluded by declaring that anyone who felt the urge to talk should speak to one of the commanders and hinted that there were professional means of assisting them. Then we all left on a brief home leave.

My parents, who had heard on Saturday night that I was coming home, raced north to save me a few hours. They took me in their car, reaching home at two in the morning. They welcomed me warmly, eager to hear about the events of the past week. I gave a brief account, omitting some of the most difficult and dangerous moments. My father was interested in the details of the battles, the operations we were assigned, and how the soldiers had functioned. My mother was more interested in what had happened to me, how I felt, and which were the most difficult moments for me. Tired as I was, I talked all the way, answering my parents' questions. It was good to return home to the family, even if only for a few hours. I gained strength from the family's support and the love they showered on me. Home, at times like these, is a haven, an island of stability in a turbulent ocean.

On Sunday morning, I paid a condolence call to the bereaved Merchavia family in the town of Eli, where I met up with Maru Gete, the commander of the First Platoon. He and I had served together with Amichai in the Hesder Unit. After a short time, Itamar Katz joined us, a company commander who now took over as representative of those of us from Bint Jbeil who had come to comfort the family. He described in detail the course of the battle from his perspective. Moshe Merchavia, Amichai's father, listened to every word, absorbing each detail. I recounted to Moshe and his wife Tova how I had come to know Amichai, and described to them some general aspects of the operation. I was particularly moved by a story the father told concerning his son. It seems that Amichai had had a serious problem with one of his soldiers who was reluctant to go into Lebanon, requesting to be excused as he was recently married. The Bible states specifically that during the first year of marriage a man is exempt from going to war: "When a man hath taken a new wife, he shall not go out to war...but he shall be free at home one year, and shall rejoice his wife whom he hath taken."

Many explanations have been given. Some commentators have argued that the Bible attaches special importance to investing in the happiness of the individual in such circumstances, despite the general requirement of going to battle. Others maintain that a husband's longing for his new wife is liable to prevent him from fighting efficiently and might even weaken the resolve of his fellow men. Amichai had helped the soldier considerably during the period of his wedding, since setting up a home was so important, but now he needed to persuade him to go out to fight. He took him to the camp synagogue and opened before him Tractate Sota of the Mishna: "When does this ruling apply? In a war undertaken by choice. But in a war for the defense of the country, everyone is required to go to battle, even a bridegroom fresh from his wedding."

He explained to the soldier that in times such as these one must rise above one's feelings for the sake of the community, as Maimonides declared: "Once he leaves for war…he must not be afraid, nor think of his wife and children, but must clear his mind of all but the battle." Amichai then, in the soldier's presence, contacted Rabbi Eyal Karim, the head of the legal section of the Military Rabbinate, who spoke to him in a friendly way, trying to encourage him to go into battle. However, the soldier remained unconvinced.

Amichai had misgivings about the incident and consulted his father a few hours before entering Lebanon. It was their last conversation. Moshe told him that in moments of crisis for Israel, the general good is more important than the individual. In such situations, important though the individual may be, together with consideration for personal needs, the plight of the country takes precedence. Finally, Amichai had to order the soldier to prepare fully for the mission, like all his friends, but said that at the moment before crossing the border he could still, if he wished, ask permission to quit the operation. Amichai wanted to put pressure on the soldier to acquiesce, but did not want to create an impossible conflict. He knew that even if the soldier decided to withdraw, the negative impact on the entire department would be small, but excusing even one soldier from action could damage morale, apart from reducing the number of men in the platoon. Amichai tried to take into account the needs both of the public and the individual, and to minimize the damage as far as possible. I felt invigorated after the visit, especially admiring the strength of spirit emanating from the Merchavia family.

Moshe and Tova Merchavia, Amichai's parents, had been among the founders of Ofra, the first village established in the Binyamin area in Samaria. Amichai was born in Talmei Yosef in the district of Yamit where they lived for eight months. Later the family helped found the village of Eli in the Binyamin area, where they raised ten children. Two weeks after Amichai fell in battle, his older sister, Emuna, got married. Moshe spoke at the ceremony, saying: "Today's wedding is taking place within the thirty-day mourning period for Amichai, a day that merges grief and joy. This is a complex world producing mixed emotions. But they do not cancel each other out; on the contrary, the joy of the wedding will be augmented and further sanctified, because in the midst of our grief we know deep within that Amichai, who looked forward so eagerly to this wedding, will, in his own way, be rejoicing with us here today." A few days after his daughter's wedding, Moshe Merchavia returned to serve in the reserves, to which he had been called at the beginning of the war.

After visiting the Merchavia family, Gete and I paid a condolence call to Sarah, Roi Klein's widow who also lived in Eli. We had become acquainted with him in joint campaigns in Gaza, where Roi was our direct commander. We told her how Roi inspired us with confidence in Gaza by his personality and calm control. We did not know then that Roi Klein would become a legend, a symbol of heroic self-sacrifice, the Golani commander who threw himself on a grenade to save the lives of his soldiers.

We left the mourners. One of the most difficult tasks for an officer is meeting with a bereaved family. There are no words adequate to bring comfort but, beyond that, there is a feeling of guilt for a soldier whose life has been placed in your hands. Parents had relied on you to bring him home safe and sound, and you returned empty-handed. I was grateful that none of the soldiers under my command had been killed, but I felt the burden of responsibility placed on all of us to bring the troops home safely.

I planned to visit the wounded at Rambam Hospital, but due to lack of time we had to drive to Jerusalem, from where my father and my sister Shakked drove us directly to the military cemetery in Haifa for the funeral of Assaf Namer, the final funeral of those who had fallen in the battle in Bint Jbeil. As we reached Haifa, the sirens sounded and a barrage of Katyushas fell on the city. We stopped the car and took shelter in the basement of a building. Gete and I were calm, probably because we were accustomed to hearing explosions and falling missiles, but my father said we should wait a few more minutes to be sure, before returning to the car and driving on.

When we reached the cemetery, I left my father and Shakked. I felt their eyes follow me as I walked away. They said nothing, but I knew how hard it was for them to leave; who can measure a parent's concern for a son? We did not know when and in what circumstances we would next meet. Ironically, it would turn out to be in Haifa – in the hospital, after I was wounded.

I joined the large crowd that had gathered at the entrance. This funeral was attended by most of the battalion, and some of the wounded were allowed to leave the hospital for it. We had not participated in the other funerals, as they had taken place while we were fighting in Lebanon. There was no time to console the bereaved families of Alex and Idan whom I had known from my days as a squad commander in November 2003. Alex had been a platoon commander in a parallel unit, and Idan a soldier in my platoon.

War has its own rhythm.

Chapter Seven

Entering Maḥibab

Monday, July 31, 2006–Friday, August 4, 2006

That night, after the funeral, we drove to Kala, a base in the northern Golan Heights, to prepare equipment for the company. The Golani Brigade was assigned to the 162nd Brigade, the "Steel Division" under Brigadier-General Guy Tzur. Monday was spent in preparations for reentry into Lebanon. We were due to carry out an urban ambush, so most of the equipment was specially designed for the task. My flak jacket was packed full. I had both shrapnel and smoke grenades, magazines, helmet and water bottles, binoculars, night goggles, a mobile radio, a GPS, camouflage netting, a knife, colored stick-lights, rubber tourniquet, intelligence aids, and more. It was hard to find room for my *tefillin*, but I knew I could not leave them behind.

That evening, the mission was changed, and the unit's officers, gunners, and drivers were ordered to the Shushan base to equip our vehicles and wait there. The next day, Tuesday, the rest of the company joined us. Having received initial orders to enter Mis-Al-Jbeil, we studied the maps and aerial photographs, after which all the officers went together to survey the area. Mis-Al-Jbeil is very close to the border, a distance of only about five hundred meters, so it was easy to identify the projected entry route. We surveyed the village from the Rakefet observation post and from others. Each officer identified the building he had been assigned to capture. We thought that at least in this operation the task of navigation and orientation would be simple, as we were viewing it in the daytime.

Navigation was one of the military tasks that I found most exciting and enjoyable. From an early age I had loved hiking, and had learned to map out a terrain. In the army, it was particularly important and challenging. I remembered that in the orientation courses I had attended during officers' course, I had found navigation especially appealing as it consisted of hiking on one's own. Darkness surrounds you as your feet lead you toward your destination. Lowering the volume on the communications radio, you enjoy the silence – just you and the hills. You feel the ridge at your feet and climb upward, and then descend a steep decline to the wadi. At a fork in the path, you take the right, and discover the coordinate, spray-painted onto a rock. Your mind plays back the route you had studied, the directions to be followed, together with the topography of the area, until it indicates a route leading to the desired goal. Navigation is important above all in helping one become familiar with the terrain, to reach the target and to analyze the dangers that threaten; but it is also important in building self-confidence, acquiring the ability to make decisions, and imposing self-discipline. You must build an effective route, plan the timing, determine the pace, and establish breaks, and yet maintain self-control – not to open a map or, Heaven forbid, copy landmarks from a colleague. Moreover, one must never despair or omit points along the way. There are further elements involved, such as walking along a concealed path, attacking at an angle, and synchronizing with other forces. On dark nights, I felt at home, even though I could see nothing. I knew exactly where everything was and where I was walking.

At the end of the surveillance, we rejoined the men at the Shushan base. We held an exercise with full equipment, including flak jackets and everything we were due to carry, such as backpacks containing bottled water. The training was designed to familiarize us with the stages of urban ambushes as well as to practice carrying considerable weight. That specific training was still fresh in the minds of the soldiers from the period in Gaza. I ordered one of them to lie on the ground as if wounded. The soldiers loaded him onto a stretcher, and practiced evacuating him to an imaginary helicopter, and then carrying him back to the vehicle. After the exercise was over, I felt from looks exchanged among the men that, to put it mildly, they had not enjoyed the exercise, so I explained to them how important it was. Only during the fighting did we all realize how essential that training would prove to be.

We again stayed overnight on alert at the Shushan base. On Wednesday, we were given a new mission. The First and Second Platoons belonging to Maru and Achikam, under the command of Gal, drove to the Blida area and took up defensive positions in one of the domes. My platoon, with Emmanuel Yushpe, the deputy company commander, under the command of Eli Michelson, the deputy commander of the Fifty-Second Battalion, was due to join up with the Golani Reconnaissance Battalion at the village of Maḥibab. We parked our vehicle in the makeshift parking lot, near the observation point, where we held briefings and prepared for action. Because the transports were not yet ready and through lack of time, we drove along the asphalt roads and I gazed ruefully at the deep ruts left in them by the tracks of both the tanks and our vehicles.

I pulled out of my kitbag the hiking map of the trail area. I had taken care to bring it from home to help me get around, and perhaps in the naive hope that I could hike along one of the routes marked on the map. I identified our position on the slopes of the Naphtali Hills. My eyes focused automatically on the paths, at the many places where I had hiked in the past, and those I had yet to tread upon. The Ḥula Valley unfolded before us to the east. The spectacular landscape was heavy with the smoke spiraling up from the many fires that were raging. I had walked here so many times, but it had never occurred to me that I would come here in uniform, wearing battle equipment, on the way to war. I promised myself that, when the fighting was over, the smoke had dispersed, and the sounds of war had died down, I would come back, returning to the magnificent panoramas of the Galilee and Mount Hermon, their flowering pathways and rushing rivers.

The sun was sinking. It was the eve of the 9th of Av. According to the Mishna Taanit 5:6, five calamities had occurred on this day: Our forefathers in the wilderness had been deprived of the right to enter the Holy Land, the First and Second Temples were destroyed, Beitar was captured, and Jerusalem was laid waste. I hoped that on this retributive day we would suffer no further disasters.

At dusk, we left in a convoy of tanks and armored personnel carriers led by a bulldozer, in the direction of the village, Maḥibab. The journey to the outskirts of the village went smoothly, but a short distance before the village, we encountered difficult terrain that limited maneuverability. I directed the vehicle carefully, attempting to avoid ditches, but we became stuck. Shifting into reverse and accelerating failed to help. I radioed for bulldozer assistance, and, with the help of our tow cable, we were pulled free. This scene of the bulldozer pulling vehicles clear was repeated a number of times, but each time it meant that afterward a soldier had to leave the armored vehicle to replace the tow cable, at which time the soldiers in the other vehicles watched intently, ready to respond if he was attacked.

In the village awaiting our arrival were units of the Golani Reconnaissance Battalion, the anti-tank unit Orev, and the Engineers and Demolition Unit. The ascent to the village from the south was very slow due to the difficult conditions of the terrain. The bulldozer cleared the way in the dark, the remaining vehicles following in its tracks, as we struggled along the rocky surface.

"To the right, to the right. Stop!" Our vehicle lurched to the side, and I was afraid it would overturn. We reversed slowly, and again continued our ascent. The engine roared as the huge vehicle overcame each obstacle. I directed the driver with the help of the night-vision equipment, but toward the top of the rise, we were assisted by infantry under the command of Elkabetz, the commander of the Golani Engineers and Demolition Unit, who came to secure our entry.

We reached the village at dawn on Thursday. At the entrance, a huge electric pylon lay collapsed, typical, we discovered, of the state of the entire village. Among the Golani officers located there were a number of friends from yeshiva high school days in Efrat. By radio I chatted with Tsachi Citroen, Gabi Grabin, and Danny Friedler.

We approached the village, and Yoav Yarom, the commander of the Golani Reconnaissance Battalion, directed us to enter, by means of an urban attack, one of the houses located between the buildings in which the Reconnaissance Unit was installed and the buildings occupied by the Orev Unit. I explained to the soldiers that we would need to rake the building with fire to clear it of terrorists, similar to the way we had entered the abandoned Syrian village in the Golan, and not like the limited conflict drill used in the West Bank and the Gaza Strip.

"What if we find civilians in the house?" asked one of the men.

"According to Intelligence, any residents who remain in an abandoned village are terrorists," I replied. But I added, "Anyway, use your common sense. If you find a baby crying in its cradle, you obviously don't shoot." I remembered an operation in which I had participated as a soldier a few years previously in one of the villages in the Ramallah area. It was a cold night, but we had been ordered to remove all the residents from the buildings. In one room I found a woman with a baby a few weeks old. She begged me not to move him out into the cold. I contacted the company commander to inform him of the situation. He, of course, confirmed that I should leave the baby with his mother in the house under guard until the end of the action. Even when there are clear and strict orders, we need to use our discretion.

I assigned each of the men their tasks for breaking in and searching the house. I instructed the soldiers who were not in the search group to provide careful fire cover along the street, adding, "Two operational essentials: One, when you exit the vehicle, don't forget to cock your weapon and make sure there's a bullet in the chamber. Two, double-check that you have two grenades in your flak jacket – we'll need them to clean out the house." I noticed some hesitation among the soldiers when I mentioned grenades. I asked why, and they said they did not feel confident enough to use them. I briefly demonstrated how to remove the grenade from its holder, to release the pin (right-handers clockwise, left-handers counter-clockwise), and to lob the grenade. All of them had thrown a fragmentation grenade during basic training, but later, as soldiers, had lobbed only practice grenades. The reason for this was probably the many accidents that had occurred in training. I decided that at some future opportunity, they needed to have additional practice with grenades. With all due caution regarding accidents, soldiers must enter battle with the necessary operational capabilities.

The break-in was effected by backing our armored vehicle forcefully against the wall of the building to make a hole large enough for entry. All the men then exited the vehicle, and we entered the building firing away. I identified a door and shouted, "There's a room to the right! I'm going to use a grenade!" Advancing to the door of the storeroom, I drew out a grenade and removed the pin. "Asael's lobbing a grenade!" I yelled, and tossed it inside, counting the seconds before the explosion, "Twenty-one, twenty-two, twenty-three... Boom!"

I entered the room, firing in all directions. A dense, suffocating cloud of dust greeted me, and I leaped back outside. The room was probably used for lumber and was covered in a thick layer of dust. We advanced to the second floor to find a long corridor leading to several rooms. The doors were locked, so we tried breaking them open by firing, but that turned out to be ineffective, so we used the break-in tool kit, smashing down the doors with a five-kilo hammer accompanied by hefty kicks. We continued clearing the rooms. Replacing my magazine, I fired into the next room. "Room to the left, using fire...Clear! Clear! Clear!"

After cleaning out the building, we placed the soldiers in guard positions. I ordered all those who had participated in clearing the house to check their personal equipment. We had brought reserve supplies of grenades and magazines so could return to full military preparedness.

Emmanuel, the deputy company commander, and I went through the building to assign positions. There was a stench from the bathroom. We looked inside and saw a hole in the floor – the toilet was not connected to a sewage system but to a cesspool in the yard. We briefed the men and began to take up positions under Emmanuel's direction, spreading black sheets along the walls, camouflage netting across the windows, and thick blankets over the door frames to prevent light from entering. On completion, and having briefed the force, we assigned positions and summarized the procedures for occupying a building. Emmanuel and I, in accordance with orders, warned that it was forbidden to take any form of "spoil" from the home, apart from military weapons. We discovered and confiscated a hunting rifle, as well as various pictures and symbols belonging to Ḥezbollah. While we were searching for weapons, one of the soldiers called me and said that he had found numerous empty cartridges scattered through the house. I replied with a smile that it was not surprising after all our firing while cleaning out the building.

That afternoon, I found a few free moments for Minḥa, the afternoon prayer, and to don my *tefillin*. Normally one dons *tefillin* in the morning, but on the Fast of Tisha B'Av, it is postponed to the afternoon. I was glad I was able to put on *tefillin* at the appropriate time, although it had not been by choice but due to the circumstances. The men ate their field rations. As I wandered around the various rooms and positions, one of them offered me some food. I recalled that I had eaten nothing since the previous night, not because of the fast, but through the pressures of action. I accepted his offer and ate; it was important to keep up my strength – who knew when we would be able to eat next?

Udi, the commander of the bulldozer, and its operator Kfir, both reservists, joined us in the building. Kfir, talkative and amusing, liked to collect Ḥezbollah flags. He said that before entering the village, he had stopped the bulldozer, stepped out, climbed the mast, and lowered the flag. In front of our building, to the east, hung a billboard with a huge picture of Nasrallah. Kfir didn't like the look of it, but of course he could not go out to remove it. Eventually, when we were leaving the village, the men shot at the billboard and ripped the picture down.

The post to the west overlooked our personnel carriers and tanks. We had left our vehicle unmanned, with its hydraulic elevator facing the hole we had made in the wall, thereby providing a safe passage to the vehicle without exposure to the street. By leaving it unmanned, we could, if the vehicle were attacked, fire back from our position without endangering anyone inside it. The post to the east occupied by the sharpshooters faced the part of the street leading to the village kasbah. All the villagers had left, and we were waiting for the terrorists to come out of their hiding places. As evening approached, the sound of explosions and gunfire increased. The village was in total darkness, as the power system, apparently, had collapsed. The night was frequently pierced by flashes of light from explosions and rockets. Inside the house, we moved in darkness, as it was forbidden to use flashlights, lest they give away our positions. We could only use either flashlights with fogged lenses or dimmed stick-lights. If anyone in the force saw a suspicious figure, they informed the others and directed fire at it. The tanks were a great help as their shelling achieved accurate hits, demolishing buildings with the terrorists inside.

Early on Friday morning, at about two o'clock, I received an update that some of our forces were moving between the buildings. One of the teams was changing its location. Accordingly, our eastern position was placed under "prohibited firing." Suddenly, Igor, one of the soldiers, called to say he had seen a figure running down the alley below his position. He had not had time to shoot and, in fact, was forbidden to shoot without permission for fear of harming our forces. I checked with the Reconnaissance Operations Officer on the identity of the character, and it turned out that it was not one of ours but a terrorist. A tank aimed at the house where the terrorist was located and after a few shells the building collapsed. According to reports from the snipers of the Orev Unit, no one had left the ruins by morning. A few days later, the Twelfth Battalion, conducting searches in the village, found the body of a terrorist. It might have been the terrorist we had detected.

Later on, I heard a report that the tank parked next to our house was shooting at an identified target. I ran to the post on the west side intending to update the men, so that they would know the firing was from our forces, but my words were cut off by a loud explosion. The firing of the tank's shell shattered the windows in our building, and a free-standing clothes closet collapsed. I leaped to it in an attempt to stop its fall but failed to reach it in time. The closet fell on Gabi's head, but fortunately the blanket covering him helped soften the blow. I then ran to the east position, where the glass had also shattered. The men shouted that there had been an explosion and flying shrapnel, but I assured them that it was not an anti-tank missile that had hit us but that one of our tanks was shelling a building from which firing had come, and that the supposed shrapnel actually consisted of glass splinters from the shattered windows. None of the soldiers was injured.

Just before first light we were ordered to leave the house and the village. We swiftly dismantled our positions and began moving out. We could not detect the route by which we had entered the village, so the deputy commander of the Fifty-Second Battalion led us out by a new route. The journey was very difficult, with numerous pits and holes along the way. After an exhausting drive, we arrived close to the border fence. Suddenly Kfir, the operator of the bulldozer, told us to stop following him for the moment. He turned, advanced a short distance, and paused in front of a Lebanese tractor. Kfir approached it, lifted it with his huge blade, and flipped it over. Then he turned and continued on his way. It was his own personal initiative, but he treated it as if it were a routine operational mission. Why did he do it? Was it an act of anger and frustration, or just a youthful prank? Perhaps he wanted to demonstrate to the Lebanese the power of an IDF bulldozer.

We crossed the border on Friday morning and stopped at an observation post to park and rest up.

Chapter Eight

Saluki

Saturday, August 5, 2006–Monday, August 7, 2006

On Friday afternoon I drove to the Shushan base to receive orders for the next operation. The mission, under the leadership of the deputy commander of the Fifty-Second Battalion, was to open a route in the direction of Wadi A-Saluki. The unit under the deputy commander of the Fifty-Second Battalion was to form the advance guard, while the main body was to be under the commander of the Fifty-Second Battalion, and to include the Second Platoon under Achikam, and Gal's armored personnel carrier. The battalion briefing ended with the onset of Shabbat and, together with Emmanuel, I returned to our company which was waiting for us at the observation point. In the forest, Deputy Battalion Commander Eli Michelson briefed all the force's commanders. As the sun set, we bent over the maps, making use of the fading light. I filled in the company, after which everyone inspected his equipment and prepared the vehicle for action.

I heard the soldiers on the vehicle chatting to each other. One of them talked about the dangers involved in the action, while another remarked that he had concealed from his parents the fact that he was in Lebanon: "Extensive training in the North," "cell phone reception problems," "low battery," and so on, with similar explanations and excuses. In their discussion of the operation, something in their voices sounded different, a lack of their usual enthusiasm. Had their tiredness and the pressures of the mission affected them? Or were they scared?

I had brought with me some laminated cards for soldiers, on which was printed a passage from Maimonides:

> "Who is the man fearful and faint-hearted?" – he who lacks the strength to withstand the pressures of war. On entering into battle, a man should rely on the Hope and Savior of Israel and recognize that he is fighting for the glory of the Lord. He should place his life in His hand and neither fear nor be alarmed. He should not think of his wife or children but remove them from his mind and forget everything except the needs of battle. (Laws of Kings and Wars 7:15)

We followed the same route as led into the village of Maḥibab, but this time we avoided the village, continuing in the direction of Wadi A-Saluki. Wadi A-Saluki is a tributary of the Litani River. It is thirty kilometers long, and creates a channel between the slopes of a ridge rising in the east and the Lebanese mountain range on the west. It empties into a basin in the south, at the foot of Jbeil-al-Caucasus (situated below Maroun A-Ras) and flows north until it joins the Litani River.

We halted the tanks and personnel carriers five hundred meters before the wadi and began preparing for an offensive. The surprise attack was designed to open an observation post overlooking the Saluki and to help secure the compound in which the vehicles were parked. The plan, to force a path that would allow the 162nd Division to cross the Saluki, was assigned to the 605th Battalion, "Maḥatz," of the Engineers.

There were still a few hours before we were due to set out. The atmosphere was tense. I talked to some of the soldiers and sensed some apprehension, partly because of what had recently occurred but partly also because of the name Saluki. That name had been seared into the consciousness of IDF soldiers as a highly dangerous area swarming with terrorists, the site over the years of a series of harsh clashes, especially in the late 1990s. The most traumatic event for the Golani Brigade had taken place on August 28, 1997, during a fierce battle between the Thirteenth Battalion and terrorists, when fire had broken out in the wadi, and five soldiers burned to death.

A small number of soldiers were unwilling to take part in the action, at first offering operational and other reasons; but as time wore on, I realized that they were paralyzed with dread. It was my first contact with open fear among soldiers. I assume that some soldiers had been afraid in previous operations, but now the anxiety had surfaced. Terror, fear of unknown dangers ahead, can be devastating for a company in such circumstances. Once it appears, it is likely to grow and spread, for fear is infectious. If not treated at the start, it can spread like a plague through the platoon. As long as fear is personal, each individual can find a way of coping with it, but if it turns into an epidemic, if it is discussed openly, it can break down the dams built to restrain it. Perhaps fear was meant originally as a protection, helping humans to avoid danger. But the situation was dangerous, we had not chosen it, and had to deal with it. Ignoring it would have compromised both the individual and the group, and would have increased the danger for the future. There was no choice, we had to suppress or overcome the fear if we were to carry out the mission successfully.

I remembered the story Moshe Merchavia told about Amichai at the condolence visit, especially his conclusion that in times of crisis the needs of the community overrule those of the individual. I realized that I had to take care of the situation immediately. I was not angry at the soldiers; I understood their feelings. We had had some difficult experiences and seen horrific sights. In other circumstances I might even have encouraged them to vent their feelings, but not when we were deep in enemy country and preparing for action. Moreover, it was not just for the common good, but also for their own good, as experiencing fear is dangerous for the soldiers themselves when in the heat of battle. After a few talks to them by the squad commanders and myself, I selected which soldiers should remain behind in charge of the vehicle and which should participate in the ambush.

After a few words of encouragement, the time had come to leave for action. We daubed our faces with camouflage, and I delivered the final briefing prior to departure. One of the men I had selected seemed to hesitate. I gave each a metal number (every soldier receives a number in case the force splits up, is involved in battle, or the mission reaches its end, when the command comes, "Check metal numbers!" Each soldier then calls out his number to ensure that all are present). On reaching the number nine, I looked up for the tenth soldier. The soldier stood up with a determined look and received the number ten. I could see from his expression that he had gone through a lot of soul searching before reaching a decision, but I believed that he would stand firm and not let me down.

We set out for the mission, due to be located on the southern ridge, walking through the night laden with kitbags and combat equipment. We stepped along quietly, careful not to stumble, and climbed the steep ascent. Emmanuel and I, searching for a suitable location for the attack, finally found two large bushes suitable for the purpose. We built camouflage positions within the bushes by pruning branches and moving rocks, in preparation for a long stay, and hurried in order to finish before first light. The posts were marked out by dawn and the men took up their positions. Five soldiers were stationed in each bush, with Emmanuel commanding one group and I the other. It was forbidden to stand up or make a noise, so we talked in whispers, and it was difficult to make oneself comfortable among the branches and on the hard ground.

We remained in the ambush position throughout Shabbat. I realized that, due to operational duties, this was the sixth consecutive Shabbat that I had not observed properly. There was, of course, the rule that preservation of life overrides Shabbat, but I missed the normal routine of prayers, blessings, a family meal, study and rest. I recalled the words of the Talmud in Tractate Yoma: "R. Shimon b. Menasya says: 'Profane one Shabbat in order to observe many!'" and I thought how applicable those words were to soldiers who desecrate Shabbat so that others can live on and observe many Shabbatot. Many Shabbat observers were now praying for our welfare in synagogues throughout Israel:

May He who blessed our fathers Abraham, Isaac, and Jacob, bless the soldiers of the Israel Defense Forces, who stand guard over our country, from the border of Lebanon to the Sinai desert, and from the Mediterranean Sea to the Arava, on land, sea, and in the air. May the Lord make our enemies flee before them. May He protect our soldiers from all troubles and dangers, from infections and illnesses, and grant blessing and success to all their actions.

Shortly after first light, the main body of the battalion arrived. Gal, together with Achikam's unit and the foot patrol, left to participate in overall security. They identified on the Al-Mafka ridge to the north of our position a hut-like structure that looked suspicious. Behind the building was an abandoned quarry and we were able to follow the unit's movements from our ridge. They attacked the structure with fire and with a LAW rocket that missed its target. As the unit approached the building, evidence was found that it had been occupied until recently. There was fresh bread and remains of food.

Suddenly, they identified a suspicious object. It turned out to be a 120 mm mortar. Next to it were some sixty mortar shells, most of them still in their packages, all of them made in Israel. It seems that it was military equipment abandoned by the IDF during the hasty withdrawal from Lebanon in 2000. The mortar was aimed toward Israel. Both it and the shells were covered with camouflage netting and straw was scattered around. Near the mortar was a box with protruding wires that the unit fired on till it exploded, in case it was a mine. After checking that the mortar was not booby-trapped, it was transferred to the parking lot, and that night, Saturday, Achikam took the mortar in his vehicle to the border. On his return, he relieved us in the attack position.

Brigade Command deliberated what to do with the mortar shells. Various suggestions were offered: to blow them up, to have tanks fire at them, to transfer coordinates to the Air Force to bomb them from the air, or to transfer them to Israel. Finally it was decided to take back to Israel the shells that were still in their packaging, and to use tank fire to destroy those that were unpacked.

On Sunday afternoon, we left on a mission to neutralize the launching pad and remove the shells. I led with an advance unit consisting of Benizri the gunner and Igor the sharpshooter. Gal, moving slightly behind me, commanded the operation. As we approached the hut where the mortar had been found, he told me to enter and look for any useful evidence. We did not know if any terrorists remained, waiting to ambush us. We moved cautiously and entered the hut firing at anything suspicious. Previously, tanks had fired shells into the area to clear it in case terrorists were still hiding there. The shed caught fire. I managed to find some electrical appliances, numerous batteries and some unidentified items, but the suffocating smoke and heat forced us out. At the same time, Avshalom joined us with an empty vehicle so that, after we had finished clearing the area, we could load the shells onto it. The Operations Officer of the Armored Fifty-Second Battalion joined us to place the unpacked shells in an exposed location. In coordination with our retreat, one of the tanks fired at the exposed shells and destroyed them.

At the end of the mission, we learned that changes had taken place in the division's plans. It was decided not to cross the Saluki for the time being, and that the engineering battalion should not force a crossing. About a week later, the 162nd Division returned to the area, and infantry and armored brigades did cross the Saluki. Fighters of the Naḥal Brigade and 401st Brigade were involved in tough battles and suffered heavy losses. Twelve soldiers were killed and dozens injured.

We prepared to return to the Israeli border. Shortly after dark, we started moving out. On the way, we stopped to load up some equipment that had fallen off a tank in the convoy. On reaching the Shushan base, we received another mission: The Twelfth Battalion and the Golani Reconnaissance Battalion were on their way out, and in the final section had to cross an area rigged with anti-personnel mines. We were ordered to arrive with empty vehicles, to pick up the men, and to take them safely across the minefield. As we drove, we heard explosions, but anti-personnel mines have no effect on an armored carrier. After a number of journeys back and forth, we returned to Shushan.

It turned out that the capture of the mortar created waves in the media. Throughout the war, no answer had been found to low-level trajectories and it was the simple, primitive mortar that caused the most damage, the IDF having difficulty in hitting the launching pads. Perhaps that was why the media focused upon the incident. Television channels continuously broadcast photographs of soldiers unloading the shells, as well as a brief interview with Gal in which he summarized the course of events. We only saw the interview after the war, online.

Chapter Nine

Operation Postponed

Monday, August 7, 2006–Wednesday August 9, 2006

On Monday morning, we moved to the hotel Nof Ginosar on the Sea of Galilee to relax, but by the afternoon were ordered out, to serve as a reserve brigade unit. We equipped the company vehicles and awaited information on the operation. The Golani Brigade was again assigned to the Ninety-First Division for action in the Bint Jbeil area, which was familiar to us. Achikam and his platoon were sent to Avivim and to transport some reserve soldiers into Lebanon. He rejoined us on completion of the task.

During the waiting period, I attempted to deal with some important matters that had, until then, not been urgent. War grants priority to certain issues, pushing others aside. Now there was an opportunity for personal chats with soldiers and squad commanders about service conditions and, with the assistance of the company medic, to deal with medical problems. The men had had a difficult time, many having had no home leave since entering Gaza. There were signs of fatigue, of mental problems, and of homesickness.

A number of volunteers who came to help residents of the north had passed through. Sometimes they gave us gift baskets, snacks, and hot meals. Chabad also visited us, distributing booklets of Psalms and blessings from the Rebbe, and wishing us success and heavenly assistance. Brigadier General Miri Regev, the IDF spokeswoman, stopped by, asking how we were, and how she could help.

Numerous text messages had accumulated on my mobile phone as well as scores of voice mails. Most were from family members and friends wanting to know how I was. I called home. A sigh of relief escaped my father's lips when he heard my voice. I tried to calm him, but could sense in his voice the disturbed nights that he had experienced. In fact, what parent with a son in Lebanon could sleep peacefully during this time? My father bade me look after myself and my men, and passed the phone to my mother, who was standing nearby. She spoke calmly, and asked if I was managing to get enough sleep. I avoided the question, saying instead that we had been receiving hot meals. I could feel her loving embrace over the telephone.

On Tuesday, we were ordered to bring supplies of water, food, maps, medical items, batteries, and other equipment to the brigade's battalions north of Bint Jbeil in the village Ainata, one of whose inhabitants was Mohammad Hussein Fadlallah, a founder of Hezbollah and also known as a spiritual leader of the organization. A large building in the village, known as "The School," served as the meeting point. The battalions were waiting for delivery before heading north. We were also to evacuate soldiers who were unable to continue in the mission because of light injuries.

One of the most difficult decisions for an officer is to determine whom to select for a mission. Operational needs are, of course, a primary concern, but one cannot ignore the fact that the decision may have profound consequences. I tried to keep the teams cohesive, and to appoint men who were suited to the task and fresh for action. But should I also consider the personal and family situation of the soldier? Ought I to have special concern for a soldier from a family already bereaved? Or perhaps for an only son, or one who is married? One squad commander, Itai, who had not participated in the last operation, offered to take my place. I refused. I could not send troops on a mission while I waited behind at the border.

We had planned to set out a little after dark, because the route was nearly eight kilometers long and we did not want to be caught in broad daylight. We were due to leave together with a tank company from the Fifty-Third Battalion reduced in size, but the tanks arrived very late, so that we were able to leave only around three o'clock in the morning. After crossing the border, the plan was reassessed and it was decided to postpone the mission, since it was clear that it would mean traveling in daylight. We turned back, deciding to leave instead the following night.

On Wednesday afternoon there was a new plan. The operations officer of the Golani Brigade, Roi Levy, called Gal, ordering him to leave earlier. It had been decided that the first part of the route, ascending the hill Al Manhala, should be in daylight; if we reached that point before dark, to wait for nightfall, and only then to continue along the second half of the route, bypassing the hill Karhabun to the north in order to reach The School at Ainata. Gal argued with Roi, asking that we wait for full darkness before leaving, but Roi said that the first part of the route was safe. Roi also explained that there were operational constraints for traveling by daylight, because the plan was that, with the help of the supply unit, the brigade should begin moving north that night in the direction of Beit Yahoun. At the meeting with Roi, Gal had expressed the fear that soldiers from the company could be hurt. In the end, no agreement was reached, and Roi told Gal firmly, "Karabaki, I am fond of you, but this is an order. That's that!"

We sat together, all the company's officers, and planned the operation and the route. We raised the issue of the anti-tank missile threat and concluded it was real, especially if we were to travel in full daylight.

The IDF had learned certain lessons during the war, and we received folders summarizing them as we approached Bint Jbeil. One section read:

Lebanon Fighting Techniques Section 2
The enemy's range of fire is immeasurably greater than in current security publications, because of Hezbollah's weapons

and strategy. If on the West Bank the range is up to a few hundred meters, in the current war, direct fire can reach much further. The organization has the capability of striking our forces accurately with advanced anti-tank missiles even while the vehicles are still traveling toward them.

The section concluded with the advice that movement during the day should be avoided.

Quite apart from this ruling, we knew that headquarters was aware of the danger, as they themselves had sent us the folders and, on the previous day, had agreed to postpone the mission because of the daylight. Moreover, that particular night was very bright, as it was the middle of the month when the moon was full.

After the meeting, Achikam asked me if I was concerned about the threat of anti-tank missiles. I told him that it was not up to me to feel pressured. We have to perform the task, and as there is no adequate response to the threat of anti-tank missiles, we must simply do our best.

The scenario of anti-tank missiles was very real for me. We had discussed it in training. I had worked out how to react in all kinds of situations in which a missile hits one of the vehicles in the convoy: how to report it over the radio, how to return fire, and how to organize the rescue. In all instances, I knew how to respond to another damaged vehicle or to treat soldiers from my own vehicle. I did not imagine an instance in which I should be the one hit.

The operation was scheduled for Tu B'Av, a day on which the Talmud states: "There were no better days for Israel than the fifteenth of Av." Among the reasons for celebrating on that day is that the deaths in the wilderness ended. I hoped that in our time too, deaths of soldiers and civilians in warfare would come to an end.

While entering the vehicle ready to leave, I suddenly felt a vibration in my pocket. It was my cell phone. I was surprised that it was turned on; probably, because the plan was to leave at night, I had forgotten to turn it off. My father was on the line asking how I was. I quickly told him that I was busy and would call back when I could.

My father of course realized that I was going back into Lebanon and asked me to let him know whenever I left or returned there, but I refused. I understood his concern, but there were security considerations. I also knew that my duties and responsibilities would not leave me time for such calls.

Chapter Ten

The Hit

Wednesday, August 9, 2006

We set out in broad daylight at 5:30 p.m. in a column of tanks from Company B of the Fifty-Third Battalion of the 188th Brigade "Barak," together with the vehicles in our company. Gal decided to minimize the danger for the force, so there were only three men in the supply vehicle. In Gal's company commander vehicle there were two more soldiers, Dima and Klich, whose presence was to enable additional response in the event of an engagement. In mine, the Third Platoon commander vehicle, there were three, Ori Zamir the driver, Ohad Peretz the gunner, and me in command.

Shortly after 6:00 p.m., after driving about two-and-a-half kilometers along the route with the signs on the armored vehicles clearly visible, we began to move north from Jbeil Beten Abdullah, to cross the road connecting the villages of Blida and Aitaroun. Who was driving in front of us? Were they returning safely from their missions? Voices on the radio interrupted my thoughts. I heard Itzik, commander of the armored platoon, who was in the lead, ask permission to cross the road and enter the outskirts of the village Aitaroun. Itzik had traveled this way the previous day and was therefore leading the convoy. I knew the route well, having studied it on the map, but had difficulty identifying the route from inside the vehicle. As long as we were inside the vehicle, we were protected from small-arms fire, snipers, and other dangers, but one could only see what was going on outside through the periscope. The angle of vision was limited, especially when on a slope, for on an ascent one could see only the sky and on a descent only the ground. I wanted to see the new area we were entering, so I decided to lift the flap and put out my head. I balanced my feet on the seat of the vehicle, stretching upward to push the heavy flap open. The dry summer air hit my face. I was conscious of the danger as I attempted to locate our position on the map as far as I could recall it. I surveyed the terrain, trying to discern the continuation of the path.

Suddenly, I saw in the distance a flash, followed by a ball of fire speeding toward us. There was no time to draw in my head. Are they aiming at our vehicle? Or at others in the convoy?

Everything shook. There was a tremendous crash accompanied by a wave of heat.

We had been hit. An anti-tank missile had hit our vehicle, precisely in the command post. It had penetrated with enormous force. The vehicle rolled uncontrollably toward the left and then came to rest. I was still standing on the seat with my head out. I felt a strange pain that I could not locate. I opened my soot-blackened eyes, looked down at the seat I was standing on, and saw in a blur my right shoe lying on the seat. Had it fallen off? Had I been hit in the leg?

I focused more clearly. The seat was shattered, as was my flak jacket.

My legs had been hit.

Some days later, I realized what would have happened if I had been sitting on the seat and had not stood up to survey the route.

Pieces of shrapnel had penetrated the crew's compartment. It was fortunate that we had piled the kitbags there instead of taking aboard any soldiers other than the driver and gunner.

But what had happened to them?

"Ori and Ohad, are you OK?"

Ori, who was in the driver's seat, reported that he was fine. Ohad in the gunner's place had received some shrapnel in his legs and his eyelids had stuck together in the heat.

"I see everything blurred but I can function."

Ohad fired a long burst from the machine gun, although unable to identify the target. Ori looked at his hand and thought that he had lost a finger, but Ohad pointed out that, though the finger was broken, it was still attached. The automatic fire-extinguishing system now turned on, spraying the interior of the vehicle.

I tried to get through on the radio. I reached up to my helmet and pressed the radio button to contact Gal: "Bungalow Three here. We've been hit by an anti-tank missile!"

"This is Bungalow Three again. We've been hit by an anti-tank missile. Need help. Over."

But there was no answer. My helmet had been damaged and the radio disabled. However, as we were the only vehicle that had failed to answer, the rest of the unit realized that it was our vehicle that had been struck. Achikam had also seen the launch of the missile but had not perceived that we had been hit. However, when he saw the smoke spiraling up from our vehicle, he reported over the radio: "Bungalow Three has been hit."

The commander of the armored company, Evyatar, had the tanks form a protective circle around us, while Gal arranged inner protection by deploying his armored vehicle and a number of soldiers. The tanks fired shells and bursts of machine-gun fire in the approximate direction from which the missile had been launched, and sent up smoke bombs to shield the vehicles from further missiles. We were in an agricultural area with houses placed far apart, and a terrorist cell was no doubt hiding in one of them. From the time of the first missile, fire had rained down on us non-stop, both rockets and machine-gun fire. Evyatar yelled, "These aren't Independence Day fireworks! Take up positions and return fire!"

After I had assured Ori and Ohad that rescue was on the way, I felt a burning heat in the upper part of my body and a severe pain in the lower. I asked Ori to try to get my portable radio out of my flak jacket. I could not do it myself because I was using my hand to support myself in a standing position. The jacket had been torn to shreds and scorched, but Ori finally managed to pull out the radio. Meanwhile, Ohad brought out a bottle of water, and the three of us drank. Before I could turn on the radio, Achikam arrived and, jumping out of his vehicle, asked how we were. I informed him that Ori and Ohad were fine but that I had been hit in both legs. Achikam tried to open the elevator ramp at the back, but I called to him that it would be better to use the deck, as the back of the vehicle was full of equipment. I told Ori to bring out the stretcher, but he had not realized I was hurt: "Why do you need a stretcher?" I did not answer.

Ori could not get the stretcher out as it was blocked by the piles of equipment. Achikam came on board, and, after failing to get me out alone, called for help from his gunner, Chen. Together they pulled me out, placing me on a stretcher brought from another vehicle. Achikam held my upper body and Chen my legs, which he arranged carefully on the stretcher. Then Achikam lowered the stretcher down from the vehicle, with Karabaki and Chen holding it from below. Dima and Klich helped carry it. Emmanuel instructed his driver, Igor, to remain in their vehicle, and came with his gunner, Gabi, to help.

During the removal from my vehicle, I saw that I was losing blood and asked them to fix a tourniquet. I do not know how, but the men said that I gave the instructions calmly as if I were not the injured person and not in the middle of a battlefield. It seems that in situations of real danger, the human mind can be surprising. Emotions can wait till the pressure is off.

Ori and Ohad were able to exit the vehicle independently. Ohad's exit flap had been smashed, so he exited through mine. Ohad was also put on a stretcher, which Emmanuel, together with Dima, placed in his vehicle.

Evyatar, the deputy company commander, ordered tank 1B to approach to evacuate me. Matan, the tank commander of 2A came on the radio to say that he had a medic aboard. Evyatar, on hearing that, because of the seriousness of my wound, canceled his order to tank 1B and ordered tank 2A with its medic to evacuate me. After several unsuccessful attempts to fit my stretcher into the tank, I was transferred to a canvas stretcher more suited to the task.

During the process, my right leg, which had been partly detached, slipped off the stretcher and was left dangling from the thigh. I called out to Chen the gunner, and asked him to put my leg back on the stretcher. Chen did not hesitate, taking the mangled leg and lifting it back, adding that my leg was "hanging by tendons, not really connected." They put me in a tank on the canvas stretcher, with Omer the medic resting my legs on an ammunition box, both to reduce bleeding by raising them, and through lack of space. The tank drove in reverse, failing to notice Ohad on the stretcher. Ohad, with the assistance of another soldier, managed to roll off his stretcher and avoid being crushed.

The tank tried to reverse once more, but one of the vehicles was blocking its way. Matan yelled to the driver to clear the way but his voice was drowned in the confusion. Finally, he turned the tank on the spot, ramming the damaged wing of my vehicle, and managed to rejoin the main arrival route. I received initial medical treatment in the tank from Omer, the loader who had been trained as a medic. Nitzan the gunner passed him the medical equipment from the medic's jacket. During the journey, Omer tore off the remains of my uniform from my legs and applied a Russian tourniquet to stop the bleeding. Nitzan pressed on one of the arteries during the journey to help the tourniquet, while Omer checked for other injuries. Omer had not managed to put on rubber gloves and was still wearing his fireproof gloves. He was crouched on his knees while inspecting me, so that the rocking of the tank threw him from side to side, banging him against the walls. Also, he could not hear me through his helmet, so he removed it. He told me afterward that throughout the journey I had tried to calm him, saying, "Don't worry, everything will be OK!" The turret could not be turned in the direction of travel because I was in it, so Nitzan, free from his duty as gunner and Omer as loader, could take care of me.

During this time, a fire broke out in the compound, apparently as a result of the shooting and smoke bombs. Emmanuel tried to put it out with a portable fire extinguisher from his vehicle. Achikam entered the damaged vehicle, sat in the driver's seat, put it into reverse and backed up, to move it away from the burning area. How often had we practiced evacuating the wounded, and here it had become real.

We began moving toward the border. Two tanks went first, to rescue me as quickly as possible, Tank 1B leading, and 2A behind, carrying me. Matan, the tank commander of the second vehicle, instructed Shoham the driver to drive quickly but carefully, as jerking could cause pain. At every bump my leg spurted blood. But the main difficulty for me was my inability to control events or even to know where we were. I was fully conscious and my thoughts were occupied with the rescue effort, trying to figure out if we were on the right route and whether there were other casualties. The condition of my legs or the extent of my injuries did not concern me at that time.

We passed by a right turn. Then we reached a mound of earth that reminded Matan of the correct way; we had missed the turn. Matan moved up to the other tank and informed them that we needed to turn to the right. Tank 1B wheeled around, passed 2A and sped up the proper trail, leaving behind a huge cloud of thick dust that obscured the view.

Boom! The entire tank shook with the force of the blow. The tank had fallen into a pit, its speed suddenly halted. It was fortunate that I was tied to the stretcher. The crew suffered bruises from the sudden stop. Matan checked out the situation and, having confirmed that no one was seriously hurt, ordered Shoham the driver to move the tank out of the pit very carefully. The tank climbed out; apparently there was no serious damage. Ori, despite his injury, drove Achikam's tank due to lack of drivers.

One of the crew from Gal's vehicle, Klich, took command of the personnel carrier, and Chen returned to his task as gunner. Ohad was evacuated in the company commander's vehicle. Effi drove fast, while Nati the gunner gave first aid to Ohad. Achikam and his driver Dror drove the damaged vehicle, even though the communication system was not working. The front of the vehicle was almost completely burned, and stained with soot and blood. As it had suffered many technical failures, it arrived at the border some time after the wounded. Throughout the journey from the area of the event to the border, tanks of Company C of the Fifty-Third Battalion spread out, responding to the sources of fire and providing cover for our convoy. Artillery was also used to cover our movements. The First Platoon commander's tank broke down through a technical malfunction, but the deputy commander of the Fifty-Third Battalion came to his assistance.

We reached the gap in the border at Malkia through which we had come originally, where a skilled medical staff was waiting. Treatment and evacuation took place under machine-gun fire and with missiles flying over our heads. Paramedics arriving at the scene along with tankers attempted to extricate me from the tank on the stretcher, but something stuck, preventing the stretcher from being moved. They tried to remove me without the stretcher by pulling the top half of my body, but to no avail. Then they saw that the stick on one of my Russian tourniquets had jammed in a shell casing. They carefully released it and took me out on the stretcher.

Due to the constant firing, the helicopter was not allowed to land, and so the wounded were transferred to ambulances. I was placed in an army ambulance containing medical staff, and Ohad in a civilian ambulance. After the tourniquets had been applied, I had still experienced pain in my right leg although, according to what I had learned, there should be no pain once the tourniquets were in place. I told the medical staff at the border. The doctors treating me – Tal Salamon, a vascular surgeon, and Oren Ben-Lulu, an orthopedist – decided to open the artery blockers and sponge my legs with two liters of "Hartman" fluid. They put a rubber tourniquet on my right leg below the knee and bandaged the wounded area. They did so on the assumption that, on reaching the hospital, the leg would be amputated, at least from below the knee. In retrospect, their decision saved my right leg from amputation. The left leg was bandaged without a tourniquet. After stabilizing the situation, they transferred me together with Ohad to a Black Hawk helicopter waiting on a makeshift landing-pad on a somewhat elevated road, and therefore protected from fire. One of the pilots approached Ohad and asked if he wanted anything. Ohad, who was dazed after shots of morphine, replied, "Yes, your sunglasses."

"Remind me when we land," the pilot replied. Ori was brought to the helicopter just before takeoff, his injury not having been recognized until our arrival at the border. After he had been placed aboard, the helicopter flew us directly to Rambam Hospital.

Rehabilitation

Chapter Eleven

Saving the Leg

T he war in Lebanon was over for me; I knew that I would not be returning to battle. But now there was a new and very different battle before me, no longer against a defined enemy, against Ḥamas or Ḥezbollah terrorists, but a fight for life: to recover from my injuries, to overcome infection, to survive surgery, to deal with pain, to learn to walk again, to return to life.

As the helicopter took off, I realized that for me, the task was over, an end to warfare, and the beginning of a new phase of lengthy medical treatment and prolonged rehabilitation. The idea was not unknown to me. Two years previously I had injured my hand, tearing three tendons, and needed lengthy treatment and rehabilitation, so I imagined that I knew the procedure.

We reached the hospital, where they removed me from the helicopter on a stretcher. I could hear the swish of the propellers and saw people running around me. Medical personnel rushed me on a wheeled stretcher for treatment, in the course of which Dr. Shani, the contact officer for the wounded, asked me for my army number and my parents' telephone number. I was then taken to the operating room. I do not remember the exact time, but the X-rays from the operating room were marked 7:30 p.m., so I must have reached the hospital a few minutes before that. The rescue had thus taken only a little over an hour from the moment of injury to arrival at the hospital, a remarkably short time.

The doctor asked me about my injury. I informed him that I had been hit by a missile, and told him what I had seen and felt, that my right leg was shattered, the left leg hit by shrapnel, and that I had burns on my hands and face. There were clots of blood around the wounds and on the stretcher, and my skin and uniform were charred. I was anesthetized for surgery. Due to the critical condition of the right leg the doctors were unsure whether to amputate it or attempt to save it. Afterward I learned that, after considerable discussion and hesitation, the second option was chosen. The leg was defined as "requiring amputation" but the orthopedist, Dr. Lerner, insisted on trying to save it despite its severe condition and the small chance of success. The two surgeons (Dr. Lerner and Professor Sudri) set both legs into external splints, inserted special nails into the bones above and below the fracture, treated the many wounds, and bandaged them as well as the burns on my hands. Ointment was smeared on my charred skin.

After surgery, I was sedated and remained in intensive care for forty-eight hours, registered as "seriously injured." In addition to the injuries described, I had also suffered significant blood loss (needing nine units of blood), and shrapnel had penetrated large areas of my body.

Ohad, whose face had been burned, and who had suffered a shrapnel injury, was defined as "moderately injured," and Ori as "lightly wounded," having broken a finger. They were both transferred to Soroka Hospital in Be'er Sheva, near their homes, and released several days later.

It turned out that we had been hit by an American TOW missile known as "Orev" in the IDF. It was not new, but was employed by many armies and terrorist organizations because of its reliability. Its range was three kilometers or more, and it was a wire-guided missile, optically tracked from launch to target. Its warhead was hollow, creating a metallic jet ("Liner") designed to penetrate armor.

After the incident, Karabaki gathered the rest of the company near the entry point, remarking that such is war, and such are the rules of the game. In a few hours, they would be going in again to complete the task. After some reorganization, Maru Gete, commander of the First Platoon, replaced me, and the convoy set off again into the night. On the way, it passed the place of the recent incident, the ascent to Jbeil Beten Abdullah, which the soldiers now referred to as "Asael's hill."

After a short drive, one of the tanks reported that it had identified an anti-tank squad. Through the thermal viewer, two terrorists could be seen crawling along the ground. On receiving permission to fire, the tank launched a shell, hitting them both. Were they the squad that had fired at me? Hard to know.

The convoy traveled at night to the rendezvous at Ainata, but because of the damage to the convoy, it was decided to transfer supplies to the brigade units by air. Eventually, however, they relied on those available. The use of airplanes endangers the ground forces when picking up the supplies, as well as causing risk to the crews themselves, as occurred three days later, when a helicopter was shot down over Lebanon, and its crew of five killed. It was also possible to move supplies by a special mobile unit, with off-road vehicles and skilled drivers moving at night without lights. However, the amount of supplies that can be transferred that way is significantly lower than that brought by an armored personnel carrier. The alternatives available to the brigade were air supply or use of the special mobility unit. The disadvantage of these methods, beyond the risk to the airmen and the limited amount of supplies from mobility vehicles, is the brigade's reliance on others. It is difficult to move a brigade when it is dependent on external factors, unsure whether priority will be given to it or to some other unit.

I woke up for the first time after the anesthetic on Friday, August 11, 2006, to find my family gathered around my bed in the midst of welcoming in Shabbat. I opened my eyes and was happy to see them. It was a joyful and exciting moment for them. To be honest, I was dazed and remember that episode only vaguely. From what I was able to recall, I was under the impression that I had lost my right leg. My mother told me later that as I opened my eyes I said: "Ima, don't worry, I'm strong!" My parents understood from these words that I imagined I had lost my leg, and hastened to assure me that my leg had, as yet, been saved. I was probably too hazy to absorb their words. Only the next day, on Shabbat morning, did I wake up completely, to find my father by my bed. My father was silent. I thought he was having trouble telling me of the new situation, telling me explicitly of the amputation, so I tried to help him and told him that I had seen the condition of the leg and understood the situation. While I was sedated, my father had spoken with the medical staff who were treating me, and realized immediately that I thought my leg had been amputated. He hastened to tell me that my leg had been saved and that the doctors had decided not to amputate. My father told me later that I seemed indifferent, apparently failing to grasp the fact.

I asked at once about Ori and Ohad, and was relieved to know that they were in stable condition. One of the most difficult situations for an officer, at least in my opinion, occurs when his soldiers are wounded in battle. There is a feeling of guilt even if, from an operational viewpoint, he was not responsible, even if the injury took place outside his area of control. My feeling is that the parents have left a valuable possession in our hands, and we must do everything to return him healthy and unharmed.

My next question was where my *tefillin* were. I remembered that they had been with me in the vehicle. My family had no idea what had happened to them, but they assured me that while I was unconscious, they had taken care of the matter; my twin brother Boaz had placed his *tefillin* on my arm and head while I was asleep. At that time, he was serving in the Jordan Rift Valley as platoon commander of a group of recruits, and, early in the morning after my injury, had received permission to visit me in the hospital. Many people asked him if he had felt anything when I was wounded. From childhood, Boaz and I had been close friends but we had never possessed telepathy, and Boaz had not felt anything special when I was wounded. For those seeking mystical elements, when Boaz reached the hospital, he discovered an infection in his right leg, the leg I had almost lost.

After having been operated on during the night of my arrival at Rambam hospital, I remained in the intensive care unit for three days, my family members taking turns at my bedside. On waking up on Shabbat morning, I tried to read the morning prayers but the burns around my eyes prevented that, so the family read them to me. They also read me the Torah portion for the week, which concludes:

> If ye shall keep all these commandments which I command you, to perform them, to love the Lord, to walk in all His ways, and to cleave unto Him; then will the Lord drive out all these nations from before you, and ye shall inherit greater nations and mightier than yourselves. Every place whereon the soles of your feet shall tread shall be yours: from the wilderness and Lebanon, from the river, the river Euphrates, even unto the uttermost sea shall your coast be. There shall no man be able to stand before you: for the Lord shall lay the fear of you and the dread of you upon all the land that ye shall tread upon, as He hath promised you. (Deut. 11)

The commentators explain that "from the wilderness and Lebanon" means from the Sinai desert in the South to Lebanon in the North. I had traveled a long journey of late, from the fighting in Gaza and the Sinai border to the fighting in northern Lebanon.

In fact, "from the wilderness and Lebanon."

I reviewed in my mind the period of the injury and rescue, remembering things in due order, a kind of video of events running through my thoughts. I was asked many times what I had felt when I realized that a missile had been fired at me. Scenes from my life did not flash before my eyes, as people have claimed in similar situations. I simply remember being focused on the rescue mission, reporting over the radio, and giving orders to the soldiers.

My family had received the news of my injury through Maru Gete, who took over from me when I was wounded. Maru in those days was dating my twenty-two-year-old sister, after I had introduced them some months earlier. I had known him from yeshiva days, we had served in the army together, and were platoon officers in the same unit. His unique personality, his determination, and his easy-going nature made me think that something positive could come of their meeting. I was a little hesitant at first because of Maru's very special history. He had come to Israel from Ethiopia at the age of eight, having been a village shepherd, not knowing how to read or write. He moved to Israel shortly before the large-scale Ethiopian immigration, Operation Solomon, and his integration had been amazing. Despite my misgivings, Shakked readily accepted the suggestion. Over the years, she had been very active in the absorption of Ethiopian immigrants and she had learned to speak Amharic impressively. I thought Shakked and Maru could manage well together, free from color prejudice. Bridging cultural divides is a challenge, but it can be overcome with willingness and openness. It turned out that my sister agreed with me.

After I was wounded, Maru called Shakked and told her I had been hit in the leg by shrapnel, but was conscious when lifted onto the helicopter. He downplayed the severity of the injury. Shakked at once called my mother to tell her the news, not imagining that the situation was worse than she had heard from Maru. My parents were in Jerusalem, and raced to the North. They were together with friends, who refused to allow them to drive under the circumstances, and drove them to the hospital. At first, my parents felt relief that, although injured, I was not seriously hurt, and had, at least, emerged alive from the inferno.

While traveling along the toll road, Route Six, they tried to find out to which hospital I had been evacuated. The deputy battalion commander kept saying that it was to a hospital in Nahariya. Israel, the friend who was driving, mentioned that he knew the head of a department at the hospital in Nahariya, and called him to find out details. The message came back that my name was not on the list of wounded, and my parents panicked, my father suspecting that people were lying to him, trying to soften the news. My brother Boaz tried to find out where I was through the contact officer for the wounded.

Finally, my parents found out somehow that I was at Rambam Hospital in Haifa. Yael, the casualty officer of the Golani Brigade, was waiting for them, together with Dr. Shani, the officer in charge of contact with the wounded, who accompanied them to the door of the room where I was undergoing surgery. Dr. Shani assured my parents that when they had removed me from the helicopter, I was conscious and that I had even supplied my serial number and home telephone number. My uncle Shmuel was already there, together with Menahem and Yonit, an uncle and aunt from the North. Shmuel had made sure to bring *tefillin* as well as food from my aunt, Nina.

Later that night, my parents met with the orthopedists who were treating me. Professor Sudri and Dr. Lerner informed them of the state of my injuries, and described the complex plan of treatment awaiting me. They discussed a series of operations, including transplanting tissue onto the right foot, and lengthening the leg by means of screws in the bones.

My family understood the severity of the injuries. My mother prayed tearfully, but soon seemed to recover, making a sort of "inventory": my head was undamaged, my eyes could see, my ears hear, the internal organs were in place and unhurt. Thank Heaven, the severe injury was located entirely below the knees. There was no reason for me not to conduct my life as planned, or at least in a manner very close to it.

Actually, my future plans were more related to intellectual skills than physical. I cannot even imagine how I would have dealt with a head injury. What would have happened if the damaged organ had been my brain, the organ that defines who I am, the way I think, the way I deal with things, that gives me my basic approach to life, my optimism and determination? What would I have done had I lost my ability to think or my mental strength? How would I have dealt with the problem then? Would I have been able to cope? How happy I was with my lot when I thought about such injuries!

Shakked was at that time in Kiryat Shmona, volunteering to help in the treatment of those residents who had stayed in the city, and distributing food and toys to children in shelters. The City Officer sent a taxi to take her to the hospital in Haifa. Two representatives of the City Officer of Jerusalem came to our house to inform my twenty-year-old sister Carmel that I was seriously wounded, but they possessed no further information. She assured them that she already knew I was wounded only in the legs, and that my parents were already at the hospital.

In Israel, a knock on the door by such messengers is a horrific event. But there are degrees: when four come together it means a death, two mean only serious injury. My father said in retrospect that if he had opened the door unprepared for such messengers late at night, he would have collapsed before hearing what they had to say. Therefore, my father said, Maru probably saved his life by informing the family before the representatives came.

The war was not over, and barrages of rockets continued to fall on Haifa. When the alarm sounded all the medical staff and visitors were required to leave for the shelters, while the wounded had to wait in their beds and hope for the best. A situation was created in which soldiers who had survived being hit by a missile in Lebanon were likely to lose their lives if one hit the hospital where they were being treated.

A few days later, items belonging to me, such as glasses, identity tags, and a watch, all of which had apparently fallen out in the helicopter, were returned to me. They also included my personal kitbag, containing, besides maps and other reference intelligence materials, my *tefillin*. The cover, made of hard plastic wrapped in fabric to protect them from dirt and damage, had survived but had been dented by pieces of shrapnel, yet the *tefillin* themselves were intact. They had accompanied me since my bar mitzva and throughout the war, and I had made sure to put them on each day.

During hospitalization, I was frequently sent for imaging tests, including X-rays, computer tomography scans (CT), ultrasounds, and angiography tests. After I regained consciousness, I was transferred to the orthopedic ward, owing to the pressure in the intensive care ward from casualties arriving from Lebanon. As I passed through the crowded Trauma Department on the way to the orthopedic ward, I could feel even the slightest movement of my bed in every muscle and wound in my body. There were soldiers to the right and left, and beyond them even more soldiers. How many had been wounded in this war! The entire wing was like a beehive swarming with worried family members, physicians, and the groans of men who had been independent the day before and were now lying helpless and in pain. At that moment, all I wanted was to sleep, to be free of the buzzing monitors, the groans of the wounded, the blinding fluorescent lights. Just to curl up into myself and escape for a moment into a sweet sleep, free of pain.

At this stage, the main problem in the right leg was the large crater-like wounds. The doctors explained that they needed to cover the exposed bone with soft tissue, otherwise it would not survive, and discussed a complex operation involving transplanting a muscle from my back to the leg. But there was also another option, a little less complex; namely, local transplanting of tissue from the leg to cover the deep wound. Finally, two days later, the second option was chosen in an attempt to avoid surgery in the back. My family and I pinned much hope on the decision, although, in hindsight, it sounded like a mere cover-up, concealing the wound without really dealing with it, using tissue that from the start was missing from the leg. Indeed, ultimately the transplant failed due to infection, and later I had to undergo the more complex operation. Despite the disappointment, I felt that now they would confront the problem more directly instead of trying to work around it. After the failure of the local operation, I was transferred to the Plastic Surgery Department.

"Come on, soldier, we're moving you to another department," the nurse told me, pointing to a bed that looked suitable for midgets.

"You can't squeeze me into a bed that size!" I said to the male nurse who came to help me move.

"Why, how much room do you need?" he laughed. Since he was about my height, over 185 centimeters (over 6 feet), I assumed that he would have experienced the problem of finding room for one's legs in a bus, or of having the upper part of one's body protrude from a sleeping bag. And indeed, it wasn't long before he said, "Wait here, and don't let anyone try to move you, I'll find a larger bed." The tall male nurse and the female nurse started arranging my splint. The whole thing looked like a minor engineering feat, and took up half the width of the bed. It did not look like my leg, and it did not feel like my leg, at least not like the one I once had...

I was moved onto the more suitable bed that the kind male nurse had provided, and looked around. I was lying in a small room, surrounded by white walls, with a white ceiling above my head. There was a small closet, a dresser, and curtains to close off my partition in the room. I am a person who loves broad expanses and the open air, and suddenly I was trapped in a narrow, limited world. White all around, colorless: white walls, white sheets, white bandages, bright fluorescent light. The faded curtains and even the coats of the medical staff were white. I longed for the sun, the many hues of nature, and wide, open spaces.

After regaining consciousness, I had known that I needed to examine my injuries and try to assess what to expect in the future. I recognized that there awaited me many complex operations and a long and very difficult rehabilitation, whose consequences were hard to assess. I believed from the first that I would eventually walk again, but did not know what obstacles I would have to overcome in order to achieve that desirable goal. I knew that I would have to first deal with pain. Physical pain, I learned, can occur not only during invasive treatment but while bandages were being changed, in the middle of the night, or just anytime.

The problem of pain also raised the question of painkillers. My attitude in the past was to deal with pain without the use of anesthesia and sedation. That was the way I had gone through the previous injury. It was a hand injury, and during treatment I refused painkillers after surgery and during rehabilitation. But now the situation was slightly different. The Rambam medical team heard about my attitude, and one of them approached me to clarify the matter. He explained that my whole body had suffered serious injury in the war. Its energy sources were limited. The body fights with all its strength, and also invests energy in dealing with the pain. He said research had shown that the process of recovery of those with similar injuries who refused painkillers was both longer and less effective. I compromised: I agreed to take sedatives to a limited extent, provided that it was always with my knowledge. That way, I could track the type and quantity of pain medications and gradually decrease them.

I heard from some of the wounded that they enjoyed the effect of the painkillers, the light-headedness and the feeling of unreality induced, but I did not share their feelings, preferring to be fully awake and conscious of my surroundings, even at the cost of some pain. I do not claim that my approach is the right one; concepts of "right" and "wrong" are irrelevant. The point is to find the balance that works for you personally.

On one of my first days in the hospital, a member of the medical staff approached me wearing a white coat and bringing with him a specialist from another department. He announced that he was about to remove the bandages for examination. Before I could understand who he was, he had torn off the bandages from my legs, causing me severe pain. He continued working intently, while I bit my lip, trying to remain sane. The doctor, watching the incident, made some notes and left.

The next morning the nurse woke me. "Good morning. How do you feel? Ready for treatment?"

"Good morning. I hope there's an improvement. What's the treatment?"

"Changing bandages," said the nurse. A shiver ran through me and I prepared myself for a bout of severe pain.

The nurse brought a water-sprinkler, and began to untie the bandages slowly and carefully.

"Does it hurt?" she asked every few minutes.

"Should I sprinkle more water on the bandage?" she inquired before each step.

I was relieved. The treatment was not painless, but compared to last night...

After I was wounded, the company continued in action for a few more days, with Avshalom taking over my position as platoon commander. On Shabbat, August 12, 2006, it was reported that there had been further casualties in the Fifty-First Battalion. It turned out that in an accident near the village of Hadat'h, a tank had run over soldiers of the Lead Platoon of Riflemen C. Two soldiers were killed: Sergeant Yosef Abutbul (who had been lightly wounded in the battle at Bint Jbeil and returned to fight with the battalion) and Sergeant Tamer (Tomer) Amer. Two other soldiers were injured. That raised the number of men killed in the battalion to ten. On Monday, August 14, a cease-fire went into effect. Even after that, action continued until the departure of all forces from Lebanon. A few weeks later, a new platoon commander was appointed, Avichay Chezi, and the battalion took up a position on Mount Ḥermon. Throughout that period, soldiers and officers of the battalion kept in touch with me; the visits and telephone calls never stopped.

One day I heard that my company had left on a further mission in southern Lebanon. It gave me a strange feeling to lie here away from the war, while my soldiers were inside it, on the front line. I was worried about them and hoped they would leave Lebanon unharmed. During the war, I had never worried as much as I did when I was in the hospital, outside the arena of influence. I realized I was beginning to feel what it was like for parents with a son in Lebanon. A sense of helplessness and anxiety, a search for every scrap of information or sign of life. I wanted to meet the soldiers and talk to them. Of course that was not possible, as they were busy fighting in the North. I decided to write a letter to them, a sort of officer's chat. It seemed to have touched their hearts, and was widely distributed immediately. Later, it appeared in several leaflets issued by communities and educational institutions. I received many heart-warming comments, some people even sending me letters of encouragement and support, including Chief of General Staff, Gabi Ashkenazi.

My family was given a room in a hotel near the hospital. Every night someone stayed with me, while the rest of the family took the shuttle-bus to the hotel. In the morning, they returned. On the shuttle-bus, families met that had never met previously but now had something in common, concern for a wounded son. The families grew very close during the difficult hours waiting outside the intensive care unit or the operating rooms. My family held their Friday night meal in a hall near the intensive care unit, and soon a number of families joined their table. My parents shared the food with them, and began singing Shabbat songs, the others soon joining in. Sadness and tears mingled with the joy of Shabbat. Sometimes in the army too, groups had met together who would never have met under other circumstances, suddenly linked by military service and battle conditions. In the same way, the families of the wounded came together. My mother established a close friendship with several other mothers and continued to keep in touch, even though their original contact had only lasted a few days. Some days last forever.

My mother told me that when I was in intensive care, there was another casualty in an adjacent room, but something about him was different. His family was not communicating with the other families, and there was a sense of alienation. On Friday night, when my mother came to visit me during the brief visiting period, she was told by one of the nurses that there was a problem and no one was allowed to enter, adding hesitantly that one of the casualties had died. In response to my mother's expression of sorrow, the nurse explained that he had not been wounded in the war. He had jumped from a building in an attempt to commit suicide. The nurse concluded, half to herself: "How could he? In the middle of the war, when young men are fighting at the front willing to sacrifice their lives, and the wounded are fighting for their lives, how could he try to kill himself?"

Once word spread that I had been injured, the flow of visitors continued non-stop. Family near and far, my friends, as well as family friends from all walks of life, fellow students and rabbis from the yeshiva high school Neve Shmuel and the Hesder yeshiva in Ma'ale Adumim, soldiers and army colleagues, and visitors who did not know me personally but came to encourage the wounded during the war and after – everyone offered their support, coming to say a kind word, and bringing a small gift or something to eat. Manifestations of support and love poured in from all sides. Especially moving were the friends who came to visit on their wedding day, because they knew that I was unable to attend. They made me feel that I was sharing in their happiness.

There was an amusing moment when a well-known entertainer came to my bed. He assumed that I must know him, but in recent years I had spent my days at the yeshiva and in the army and so did not recognize him; nor did my father. We did our best to hide the fact so as not to embarrass ourselves or him…

My mother began two notebooks: in one, people wrote words of encouragement and good wishes, sometimes while I was in surgery or under anesthesia. In the evenings, my mother would read them to me. I found it hard to read because of the burns around my eyes, so together we went over the comments. Many people invested considerable effort in composing the message, either through kindness or because they themselves had sustained a loss. The second notebook was a diary written by my mother, documenting the events. Oren, my younger brother, wrote a poem for my recovery, which moved me greatly.

Many soldiers who had suffered leg wounds or other injuries came to visit too. One of them, Baz Mor, came to the hospital while I was asleep. He told my parents that he had suffered a serious injury while serving in Golani over a decade ago. His shorts revealed a scarred leg. Baz amazed my parents when he told them that he had come by bicycle from Kerem Maharal, a distance of twenty kilometers from the hospital. He spoke to my mother about the difficulties of rehabilitation, and told her that it was a long process with ups and downs. The point, he said, was not to despair at the "downs." They will come, but one should endeavor to be strong and wait for the next "up." As time passed, I found he was correct. The journey of recovery is indeed long and complicated, but as long as there is progress one can get through any difficulties on the way.

There were also many visits by senior officers from the army in general and from the Golani Brigade in particular. The brigade's Casualty Department did its job exceptionally well. Officers and NCOs from the section kept in touch with me throughout the period, and took care of all the brigade's wounded, offering full assistance.

There were some days when the pressure of visitors left me no time to rest. Later, I learned to create a break in the middle of the day by drawing the curtains around the bed or shutting the door. The visitors strengthened my spirit, but I also needed some privacy to rest my aching body.

In addition, my cell phone never stopped ringing, as friends called up constantly to wish me well. One of the calls was from abroad. Eitan and Margalit Ozeri from Efrat were on the line. Their son Barak had served with me in the same battalion, and we had been squad commanders in the same platoon in the class of November 2003. A year later, when he was a platoon sergeant, Barak had died at Gush Katif in the ruins of the village Pe'at Sadeh. His parents, hearing of my injury, hastened to call me and pray for my recovery. They told me of their concern on hearing I was hurt and wanted to know the situation. On their return to Israel, Eitan and Margalit came to see me together with their children, offering comfort to me and my family.

One day, while I was hospitalized in the Plastic Surgery Department at Rambam Hospital, Wageh and Hana Mansur from Isfiya came to visit the Golani wounded. Their son Nidal had joined the army in November 2003, and I was his immediate superior. I had met the family on a visit together with Nidal during that period. Later, during leave, Nidal had been killed while visiting a club. Some criminals became involved in a fight, had shot in all directions, and Nidal, who was not involved, had been hit by a stray bullet. I was in an officers' course at that time, but I paid the parents a condolence visit and did the same a few more times after that, establishing a warm relationship with them. Nidal's parents felt a deep connection with the Golani Brigade and came to visit its injured officers without knowing that I was among them, but were very moved to find me there. Wageh came over to me, and Hana, standing beside my mother wishing me a speedy recovery, suddenly burst into tears. My mother hugged her. It suddenly struck me how lucky I was to be alive, despite the severe injuries. Life had been granted to me as a gift. At the end of that emotional and stimulating meeting, they gave me, as they did the rest of the Golani wounded, a wall clock bearing the Brigade emblem, together with their wishes for a full recovery.

Many synagogues throughout the world, and for a lengthy period, offered a prayer for the recovery of "Asael Ilan the son of Yardenna Ada." Months after my release from the hospital I still met people who, on hearing the name Asael, and seeing that I was wounded, realized that it was I for whom they had been praying. My middle name, Ilan, is the name of Ilan Manns. My father had been his youth leader in the Bnei Akiva movement, and Ilan had been killed in a training accident in the paratroopers thirty years before. His parents and other members of the family came to visit me in the hospital. His brother-in-law, Major-General Elazar Stern, the head of the IDF's Human Resources, said that on the night I was wounded he had received a list of casualties. He recognized the name and saw that I was seriously injured, but had no additional information. In accordance with procedure, he did not pass on the information directly to my family, waiting for it to be reported through the proper channels of the city officer. But my family had received prior information when Gete apprised my sister, and so was actually more up-to-date, having heard that the injury was primarily in the legs and that I was conscious during evacuation. In retrospect, Stern related how concerned he was, because the term "seriously injured" includes a wide range of injuries, some of them far more serious than mine.

In the era of the Internet, news spreads swiftly and to many countries. My father, a mathematics professor at the Hebrew University, has a research relationship with many academicians throughout the world. Within days, my father's e-mail box was filled with hundreds of messages from around the world. I received wishes for my recovery from many nationalities and religions. Notable among them were many letters from Iranian scientists living in the United States, and in a working relationship and friendship with my father. Some were devout Muslims, but they also prayed for me in their mosques.

As mentioned, the local implant failed to knit and became infected. The doctors in the Plastic Surgery Department at Rambam had to remove the implant, and again expose the bones. Two weeks later, the team of doctors at Rambam, led by Dr. Lerner, recommended that I be transferred to Tel Hashomer hospital where a muscle would be transplanted from my back to my right leg by Dr. Batia Yaffe.

It was agreed that subsequent orthopedic treatment would be at Rambam Hospital, but plastic surgery and the treatment of blood vessels would be at Tel Hashomer. I was favorably impressed that the doctors preferred my welfare over considerations of prestige and competition between hospitals, and had chosen cooperation in order to achieve the best results.

My family began to collect the belongings I had accumulated during the two weeks spent in the hospital and, at the same time, they packed up their belongings from the hotel where they were staying and returned the keys. There was a sense of parting in the air, joy mixed with sadness. I was happy to leave the hospital despite the good relationships that had been established with both me and my family. On the other hand, I was going to another hospital. The road ahead was still long.

The transfer itself was very unpleasant. Every movement caused me pain as they transferred me from the bed to a stretcher, wheeled me through the hospital corridors to the parking lot, and put me in the ambulance. The driver tried to lift the stretcher as gently as possible into the ambulance, but the metal splint on my leg interfered. At last he managed to fit me in and find room for my legs. The journey in the ambulance was itself difficult, as every little bump in the road caused me great pain. In the course of the journey, I recalled how the evacuation from the tank had been even more painful. The easiest was the flight by helicopter.

Chapter Twelve

Plastic Surgery

I arrived at Tel Hashomer and, after being registered in the emergency room, was transferred to Plastic Surgery where I was assigned a room in the ward. The doctor on duty, Dr. Eli Regev, came to examine me and diagnosed a severe infection in the leg. At night, it was decided to call a senior physician, Dr. Jeremy Tamir. So, on the night of my arrival I was taken into the operating theater and, at two in the morning, had the tissues of the wounds cleaned. During surgery they had to remove part of the talus bone, in the ankle joint, due to infection.

For the next few months, I was confined to bed. It was a difficult time. A few days before, I had been an independent person, a Golani officer leading his platoon into battle in Lebanon, and now I was lying in bed, needing help for almost every action. Friends organized a shift, one of them staying each night with me in order to assist. I could not get out of bed, and needed assistance in medical procedures. Food was brought to me by tray and an electric bell was attached to my bed to call for help. These all contributed to a sense of helplessness. Gradually, I discovered ways of regaining some control over my life, from drawing the curtains in order to gain privacy when I wanted to rest or sleep, to controlling some of the medical treatment. It was important for me to be aware of what was happening. I asked what treatment I was due to undergo, what creams or medications I was to receive. I learned the forms of treatment and the dressings, the methods of intravenous infusion and the names of the doctors and nurses dealing with me. I learned to distinguish between the different antibiotics I received, to identify the components of the blood tests, to recognize the bones, muscles and tendons in my legs, and to perform many of the procedures required for myself. I came to know the various types of imaging tests. My uncle and aunt, who were both doctors, helped me understand what was happening and supervised my medical condition. My interest in the field was partly curiosity and a desire to learn, but also a need to recover some control over my life.

Every morning the nurses removed the bandages, washed my legs, and cleaned the many wounds. Doctors came to check the situation, sometimes treating the wounds themselves and sometimes giving instructions to the nurses regarding further treatment. I refused to let my family be present during treatment, afraid that the precarious state of my right leg and its dreadful appearance would cause them unnecessary suffering. I hid the leg from them throughout that period, and only months later, when the leg itself was better, did I agree to my father's request and show them pictures of the injured leg as it was during the first month after injury. On seeing the pictures, my mother admitted that I had done well in preventing them from seeing it. Looking at a photo is far easier than seeing the leg itself as it was then, especially when one could appreciate the improvement that had taken place.

Often, after examining the wounds, the doctors would decide to sanitize them by cleansing the tissue once more. The term "sanitize" sounds gentle and pleasant, as perhaps it is in sterile surgical procedures. But, in fact, the doctors applied a scalpel and other instruments of torture so that when they dug deep into my legs, the nurse wanted to give me painkillers. I never screamed, but she understood the situation from my expression and my breathing. I was asked whether

I wished to have the procedures in the operating room under general anesthesia, as when I first arrived at Tel Hashomer; that was normal procedure, the doctors claimed. But I refused. The nurses gave me a painkiller pill before treatment which reduced, if only slightly, the intense pain.

The doctors and nurses repeatedly stated that diet was an important component of recovery. On more than one occasion, the doctors' visits concluded with the categorical statement that my diet was more important than any medicines. I undertook a strict regime of eating foods high in protein and other ingredients. Proteins, I was told, are essential for building tissue – something my body needed to perform urgently. From now on, I thought of food not by name but by its nutritional quality. Meat and poultry became "protein," bread became "carbohydrate," yogurt "calcium," and fruits and vegetables "vitamins." My wider family joined in the operation, with aunts and grandmothers cooking and preparing food, and uncles and cousins bringing supplements to my daily diet. I received so many visitors bringing delicious consumables as contributions to my recovery, and in such large quantities, that I was able to share them with friends who came to see me.

One night a friend came to visit me who had also fought in the war as an officer in the Golani Brigade. He shared with me the feeling he had experienced on his way back from the army: his surprise to find that everything was continuing as normal, buses running, shops open, and people living routine lives. Business as usual! He said he could grasp it intellectually, not really expecting anything different, but emotionally it rankled. Why such a hurry to return to routine after we had so recently been at battle, burying comrades, many of us injured and still licking our wounds. For those who had participated in the war, everything seemed to have changed beyond recognition. I told him that sometimes when I entered an elevator, people glanced at my legs and asked if I had been in a car accident. When told that my injury was from the war, they were astonished: "From the war this summer? Really?" In the public memory, the war had been over for many weeks, and the country was back on track. Such is the life force inherent in the human soul. We have the ability to remember, but thank Heaven we also have the ability to forget, and to move ahead. Otherwise, we would suffer every day from deep incurable traumas. Humans have a remarkable ability to experience difficult and painful events, yet not to succumb – to emerge with heads held high.

How terrible are the lives of those men, I thought, who are unable to free themselves from memories of the battle, scenes that remain within them, keeping them constantly traumatized. The scenes are recalled continually, emerging at the slightest cause, in different forms, day and night, as images, nightmares, noises, tantrums, and outbursts, accompanied by a terrible fear that they may recur at any moment. Worst of all, those vivid memories prevent them from returning to normal life and from moving on. The more contact I had with such patients in the hospital, the more fervently I prayed that I would be spared such symptoms.

About three weeks after my injury, my youngest sister, Meitar, turned twelve. Her bat mitzva celebration had been arranged before I was hurt and, after much deliberation, the family decided to hold it nonetheless. In retrospect, the party gave added strength to both family and guests. I could not attend, but was able to congratulate Meitar by means of a brief video shown during the party. It was said that I was both absent and present. Obviously, everyone inquired how I was, wished me a speedy recovery, and mentioned me in their speeches. I stayed in Tel Hashomer hospital with friends who had come to spend that time with me. We joked that I had received an exemption from the party, while Boaz was compelled to obtain leave from the army to "meet the girls." Although it was all said with a smile, I was, of course, sorry not to be present at my sister's celebration. Nevertheless, both my family and I remained deeply thankful to Heaven that, even if I could not attend the party, I was alive and recovering from my wounds. Dates and events seemed to have a special significance that year.

The relationship between Maru and my sister, Shakked, developed swiftly. Perhaps their common concern for me added an extra dimension, and before long, they decided to marry. This time, I was able to attend the joyful ceremony and it was one of the happiest days of my life. It was, in fact, a very special experience, mingling a variety of languages and traditions. Maru wore on his forehead the "Ribbon," a red-and-white tape of symbolic significance in the Ethiopian community, the white representing the purity of marriage and the red the blood of virginity. In the evening, the Kes, or Ethiopian rabbi, conducted the ceremony, placing the ribbon on the groom's forehead. The canopy was decorated with hand-woven items, again according to Ethiopian tradition, and the dancing proved to be a fascinating mixture, the music alternating between hasidic wedding songs and traditional Ethiopian songs. The guests of the bride and groom danced together to the music. When Ethiopian music was played, Maru's family took over; the dances consisting largely of shoulder shrugs which the Israelis tried eagerly to imitate. Soon everyone was dancing in the Ethiopian way. Dancing primarily by shoulder shrugs suited me well at this stage of my life, as it did not require skill in the legs, so I was, in fact, able to dance at my sister's wedding. People stuck shekel bills on the foreheads of Shakked and Maru, again in the Ethiopian tradition. I prepared a brief performance in honor of the bride and groom. I entered the hall in a wheelchair together with a friend riding a unicycle. Holding his hand, I turned on the spot while he twirled around, all to the rejoicing of the crowd: "The sound of joy and gladness, the sound of bride and groom."

A few weeks after my injury, a new cousin was born. My aunt Zafi, my father's sister-in-law, gave birth in the Maternity Ward at Tel Hashomer. My mother and sister wheeled me in my bed to visit my aunt and little cousin (he received the name, Yuval, a few days later). Although the maternity wing is also located in the hospital, the atmosphere there is quite different. Apart from its beautiful design, it is a happy section of the hospital. People come in good cheer at the creation of a new life and not because of illness or injury. On greeting my baby cousin, I announced with a smile the start of a competition: which of us would learn to walk first.

War wounds typically suffer from infection. The type of injury, the prolonged process of evacuation, and the non-sterile area in which fighting occurs all contribute to the development of infections in war wounds. Like others, I also suffered severe infection in my right leg.

To cope with the difficult and lengthy infection, samples of leg tissue were collected, and from these tissue cultures there developed, according to the doctors, a veritable "zoo" of bacteria. The talus bone of my ankle joint had been damaged by the missile, but now I also suffered from osteomyelitis, infection in the bone itself. The talus bone is very important for bearing weight and providing mobility in the ankle joint, so that infection there is a significant risk. In order to cope with the infection, I received many antibiotics, some intravenously and some by pills. Due to the multiple transfusions I had received, it was decided to install a central line in my arm, a "PICC line," and to insert the prescribed antibiotics through the tube, thereby avoiding multiple pricks.

Apart from the festering of the wounds and the pain, the infection also raised my temperature. At least once a day my body temperature rose above 38 degrees Celcius (100.4 Fahrenheit) degrees. Those weeks were frustrating, with a heavy cloud of uncertainty threatening, beside the suffering itself. Every day we hoped the temperature would subside, but usually I felt dizzy as my temperature rose well above the normal degree level. Only a few weeks later was my body able to overcome the infection. Paradoxically, or perhaps understandably, there is a higher risk of infection in hospitals through contamination. Measures are taken to prevent the spread of bacteria, but they are not always effective, as exposure to multiple and varied antibiotics among other patients also suffering from infections spreads bacterial strains resistant to treatment.

After my body had recovered from the infection, doctors recommended that we return to the original program, a series of operations to save my right leg. Fear of amputation continued to threaten, but doctors believed that there was a good chance of saving it. The next step planned was complex surgery; taking a muscle from my back and implanting it on my leg, the muscle being used simply as a soft tissue to protect the exposed bone. It involves complex microsurgery, in which the muscle is removed together with the vein and artery, and grafted onto the leg. The downside is, of course, the damage to my healthy back, though muscle regenerates after the operation.

My family raised with the team of doctors the possibility of taking the muscle from a member of my family as they wished to ease my pain and relieve me of extra surgery. However, there was a moral problem: why damage a healthy person when the muscle could be taken from me? Why harm, for example, my twin brother who was not an identical twin and had not been wounded? Organ donations and transplants involve complicated ethical issues familiar to the medical world and to rabbinic law. In my case, however, the option was off the agenda since, as the doctors explained to us, an implant taken from my own body would bond far better than a graft from another person, the chances of success being infinitely greater than if taken from another person.

Central to the decision concerning surgery was a further dilemma. Was it better to save the leg at all costs, or to amputate it? The answer seems obvious: to save the leg at all costs; but there were weighty contrary considerations. To make an informed decision, I tried to detach myself from the problem and think rationally. First, it was by no means clear that the leg, after all the treatment, would function better than a prosthesis. Today prostheses have become highly developed, with many models and a range of adaptations. Many amputees walking around with an artificial leg are able to achieve a high performance level, including participation in competitive and challenging sports activities.

In this connection, I remembered Yoav Yarom, the commander of the Golani Reconnaissance Battalion, with whom I had fought in the village Maḥibab in Lebanon. Yoav, although an amputee from a landmine injury suffered many years ago in Lebanon, nevertheless participated in the war just like any other combat battalion commander. In my case, moreover, saving the right leg meant damaging another part of my body, so that the possible saving of the leg (a process that might not succeed) carried a price tag in the form of injury to my back, liable to impair my arm movements. Was the price to be paid worthwhile, especially with the risk that the transplant might not work? Finally, rehabilitation after amputation is short and simple compared with the rehabilitation of a leg on the verge of amputation. My leg would require numerous operations and medical treatment that would take months or even years. I was twenty-four years old. Did I really want to invest months and years of my life in physical therapy and rehabilitation for a leg that was unlikely, in any case, to be able to serve me later?

Then, there were of course significant arguments in favor of saving it. Some of these were functional, others more complex, related to the human spirit. On the functional level, a real leg, if its nerves are responsive, offers an important advantage. A prosthesis can feel nothing, while a real foot can feel the ground, whether its surface is smooth or rough, and can help the body's balance, preventing falls. Feeling the ground under one's feet, so natural to a person with two legs, is sorely missed by an amputee. Moreover, on returning to normal life after treatment, there is no need to wear the prosthesis every day and remove it at night. There is no need to carry around a second modified prosthesis for use on the beach or in the water. In short, life without a prosthesis is much less burdensome, especially for someone like me who enjoys hiking and swimming.

But beyond the practical aspect, the emotional plane cannot be ignored. A basic desire of a human being is to live with all his limbs, to experience his body in its entirety. I also learned that many people who had lost a limb had difficulty accepting the loss, even if the prosthesis provided full functionality. Many see their amputation as a physical deformity, aesthetically disturbing. They feel disfigured in their own eyes and in the eyes of others, with some of them never able to come to terms with their situation. Furthermore, an amputation is irrevocable, while attempting to save a limb still leaves choices open. To this argument is added the hope that there might be future innovations in the medical field to improve the situation.

There are considerations additional to those presented here, but I tried to keep the analysis at a substantive level. I could not restrict myself to the practical or functional aspects and ignore others. The decision was indeed difficult, and I knew I had to bear the consequences. In the end, I decided, in consultation with my family and at the recommendation of the doctors, to try to save the leg, but of course that decision is not necessarily relevant for others with a similar predicament.

Sometimes we seem to face crucial decisions, yet it turns out that other considerations take over. The doctors asked me from which back muscle I preferred to have the transplant taken – from the left, because I'm right-handed, or from the right, because it would be easier for me to strengthen my right arm. Eventually, the decision was made for reasons connected with the surgery itself. In tests conducted before surgery it transpired that it was easier to operate on me when I was resting on my left side, and thus it was more convenient to take the muscle from the right.

About a month after I was wounded, the surgery was performed by Dr. Batia Yaffe of Tel Hashomer Hospital, together with a team composed of general surgeons, plastic surgeons, and orthopedists, joined by Dr. Lerner from Rambam. It lasted ten hours, and a few hours later I woke up in the recovery room. The doctors were pleased, stating that the operation had gone smoothly. My parents told me joyfully of their satisfaction. It was hard for me to grasp their words, but the look in their eyes was enough to reassure me. However, late at night, Dr. Eli Regev saw that the implant had turned white, and called Dr. Yaffe at home. She came, studied the color of the implant, and decided, in order to increase the blood flow, to inject me with an epidural. Epidural anesthesia is generally used to lower pain, especially for women giving birth, but it also has the side effect of expanding blood vessels. In my case, the expansion of the blood vessels was needed to increase the blood flow and help the implant to bond to my leg. Since it was a surgical procedure, however simple, I was asked to sign a consent form which was brought directly from the maternity ward. I handed over the decision to my parents as I was not in a position to weigh all the considerations. After hearing the reasons for the injection and the risks, they decided in favor, but the medical staff insisted that I myself should sign the form. But the mere act of signing was difficult for me as my right hand was temporarily paralyzed because of the operation, and every movement in the rest of my body involved intense pain. My parents begged the doctors to let them sign my name, but were refused, because I was an adult and conscious and, according to the law, was responsible for my body. Finally, the form was brought near my left hand and I scribbled something by moving the fingers slightly. Following the signing, I was given the epidural and the color of the implant improved accordingly. Having learned a lesson from the incident, my parents obtained a legal power of attorney from me to prevent any impediments next time. Fortunately, we have never needed it.

In the Plastic Surgery Department at Tel Hashomer were some other soldiers wounded in the war. In the room next to mine was Moran Harel, a reserve soldier injured in the village of Debel. In that incident, nine soldiers were killed when two missiles hit a building, and Moran himself was seriously wounded, only rescued after a few hours. His uncle, former Chief of Staff Moshe (Bogie) Ya'alon, visited him frequently. I recognized him on one of his visits, greeted him, and mentioned that we had met. On hearing my name, he remembered the meeting. We were together at a memorial to Major General Nehemia Tamari, who was killed, in 1994, in a helicopter accident while he was head of Central Command. Bogie, who had been under the command of Nehemia Tamari, regularly attended the memorial services at the cemetery. My family also attended each year as Hannah, Nehemia's wife, was a relative. At the time of the memorial service five years previously, I was due for military service and wondering which unit to join. After considering many, my final choice was between navy commandos (Shayetet Thirteen) or an infantry battalion. On the one hand, service in an elite unit is prestigious, opening the possibility of making a greater contribution by participation in major operations. Its fighters are of very high caliber and are reputed to enjoy considerable satisfaction in their work. On the other hand, service in the infantry battalions means serving with people drawn from all over the country. These are units bearing responsibility for the country's safety and offering an educational challenge. Soldiers joining those battalions are not exposed to a strict selection process nor to rigid physical inspection. The challenge there for both soldier and officer is to succeed despite the social and personal difficulties and despite problems of motivation. The memorial service had been delayed, and we stood crowded around the grave, a chief of staff side by side with a novice. My father, who had known Bogie when he was chief of staff, began talking to him. I seized the opportunity, joined in the conversation, and asked his opinion concerning my dilemma. He raised a number of points, from which it was clear that his tendency was to recommend that I serve in the infantry. One of his arguments was that, although the officer potential was very high in the elite units, in practice few of them actually went to officers' school. From the long-term point of view, the army needed officers who could contribute for many years in regular and reserve service. Bogie remembered our conversation and its location, and told me he believed I had chosen correctly. I was surprised that he remembered our talk, as five years had elapsed since then. After that, he continued to call in to see me on his frequent visits to the hospital and we discussed many topics.

The High Holidays approached. On Rosh HaShana, the New Year festival, my family stayed with me in the hospital. I was still confined to bed, so they wheeled me to the synagogue. In the service we reached the prayer *Unetaneh Tokef* which, according to ancient tradition, was composed by the martyr Rabbi Amnon of Magenza as he was carried to the synagogue after his hands and legs had been mutilated. The cantor began chanting the prayer, reaching the lines:

The great shofar will be sounded and a still, small voice will be heard. All mankind will pass before You like sheep. As a shepherd counting his flock has each sheep pass beneath his staff, so shall You count, judge, and consider the souls of all living creatures, determining the lot of each and recording the verdict – who will pass from the earth and who will be born; who will live and who will die; who will end life at its destined time and who before its time; who will die by water; and who by fire; who by sword; who by wild beast, who by famine, who by thirst, who by storm, who by plague; who by strangulation; and who by stoning. Who will rest and who will wander, who will live in harmony and who will be harried, who will enjoy peace and who will suffer, who will be impoverished and who will be enriched, who will be degraded and who exalted.

As I listened to the words, a shiver passed through me. "Who by sword" – I remembered those who had given their lives in the recent war.

Many worshippers, from all sectors, wished me a speedy recovery. Together with the families of Moran Harel and Dubi Genish (a reserve company commander in the Engineering Corps with a wound very similar to mine), we enjoyed a festive meal with all the traditional symbols. We all prayed that this difficult year would be replaced by one of blessings.

A few days later I received my first wheelchair. After adjusting to it, I was able to move about more freely. Yom Kippur, the Day of Atonement, was approaching and I wished to fast, but the doctors were strongly opposed, and I realized I had to submit. Such is also the position of Jewish law on the subject, but I was sorry that I could not abstain from food and drink. I called the head of Yeshivat Ma'ale Adumim, Rabbi Rabinovich, to inform him of the doctors' decision and he replied firmly that the requirement to fast on Yom Kippur was annulled in my situation. However, instead of eating normal food, I used Ensure, a liquid providing concentrated energizers and vitamins, and drank that only in small doses and at long intervals. The doctors had agreed to that from the medical viewpoint, so by avoiding solid food, I felt as if I were fasting.

I realized that this was the fifth consecutive fast that I had been unable to observe. On the Fast of Esther, I had been in action in the Qalqilya area; on the 17th of Tammuz, I had been preparing for action in Gaza; on the 9th of Av, I was in action in Lebanon; and now, on both the Fast of Gedalia and Yom Kippur I was in the hospital, forbidden to fast. However, on Yom Kippur, I had managed to reach the synagogue by wheelchair, and that marked an improvement compared to Rosh HaShana.

My family and I hoped that I would be home for Sukkot a few days later, but shortly before then, medical treatment required me to remain under observation for several days. We were disappointed, but organized another family celebration in the hospital. Our friends, the Ziskin family, whose custom it was to hold melodic evenings with hasidic songs, suggested moving the event to the hospital on the night that ended the festival, and it was attended by many people. The event was held in a hall at the hospital, with musical accompaniment and the distribution of hasidic songbooks. The event attracted a large crowd from outside, but also from within the hospital itself, as many patients came down from the wards to participate in the exciting evening. Even within a hospital, one can experience the exaltation and joy of a festival celebration.

My first home leave from the hospital took place more than two months after my injury. It was the festival of Simḥat Torah, which occurred on a Shabbat. I traveled to Efrat by ambulance, after the nurses had instructed me on the medicines to be taken. During the journey, I was able to enjoy the view through the back window of the ambulance. We drove through the Valley of Elah and ascended in the direction of Gush Etzion. I knew the way well, having been there many times, and having gone hiking often in those areas. The landmarks were familiar, as were the names of the towns marked on signs, but it was a journey very different from previous trips. Memories raced through my mind as I came closer to home. Although I had been away for only three months, so much time seemed to have elapsed since my last visit. I arrived in Efrat to the applause and encouragement of family and neighbors, and my later arrival at the synagogue in a wheelchair was greeted with excitement by my friends in the community. The next morning, we organized a service in our home, after which I went to the synagogue where, in accordance with Simḥat Torah custom, many Torah scrolls were taken from the ark and read aloud. Everywhere I went, I was called to the reading, the many instances perhaps compensating for the long period I had been away.

The next week, when a ceremony was held to mark my company's completion of its basic training, I asked whether I could attend and obtained permission from the doctors. As I got out of the ambulance into the square at Kfar Hanassi, near Ḥatzor Haglilit, my soldiers excitedly surrounded and embraced me. I was thrilled to meet them. Although, since my injury, I had met most of the soldiers during their visits to me at the hospital, it was different seeing them completing the course together. The soldiers received their Golani insignia, confirming that from now on they belonged to the veteran companies of the battalion. The volunteer ambulance driver who had driven me throughout the day suggested we pay a short visit to the grave of R. Shimon b. Yoḥai on Mount Meron, and from there we drove to a memorial ceremony for the Golani fallen, that took place at the Golani junction. Some of the bereaved families I met there had been known to me from my army service and from the recent war. My mother, who accompanied me on that emotional day, made an interesting comment. She said that at Kfar Hanassi many parents had approached her with sympathy and even compassion for her wounded son. At the other ceremony for bereaved parents, we realized again how much we had to be thankful for. Although wounded and due for lengthy rehabilitation, I had been granted the gift of life. Whatever difficulties lay ahead, life itself was a gift.

Chapter Thirteen

Learning to Walk Again

About three months after my injury, I was transferred to the orthopedic ward at Rambam hospital for a two-week period, during which I underwent a further operation to install an Ilizarov system in my right leg. The system involved inserting metal wires into the bone on either side of the fracture, connected to rings on the outside of the leg. That system had already been installed on my left leg five days after the injury as, apart from holding the leg firm, it also compensates for certain elements that are lacking. In the case of my right foot, I needed a more complex Ilizarov in order to also lengthen the leg or, to be precise, to recover its natural length.

An adult's bone does not grow except in one instance, where there is a fracture. The inventor, a Russian Jewish doctor named Gabriel Ilizarov, took advantage of this natural feature as a means of lengthening a limb. The principle, ingenious in its simplicity, was to break the bone at a healthy point and let it grow together under control. After the bone has been broken, a system of bolts is attached with screws on the outside. By turning the external screws, the inner bolts expand the space between the broken bones; the body, recognizing the break, tries to heal it by letting them grow together. This method has been used for dwarfs, for people with malformed limbs, and for people like me who had suffered injury.

My right leg had become shortened by five and a half centimeters, and by widening the space by about a millimeter per day, or a quarter-turn of the screw every six hours, in less than two months I was able to stop further reduction. X-rays showed that the fiber between the bones was knitting together. After the leg was fully lengthened the system would have to remain in place for several months until the bone was completely mended.

The orthopedist who treated me, Dr. Alex Lerner of Rambam Hospital, had been a student of Dr. Ilizarov in Russia. He moved to Israel in the early nineties, after having been a senior doctor in his country. In Israel, he was forced to begin his residency in orthopedics from the beginning, but Rambam hospital recognized his talent and the extra professional knowledge he had brought with him from Russia. It turns out that Russia has a high standard of orthopedics, with Dr. Ilizarov inventing some unique methods of treatment over the years that were adopted in the Western world. Dr. Lerner is recognized as a world expert in orthopedic war injuries. He had had, unfortunately, extensive experience in treating casualties from Lebanon over the years. He treated me professionally and with great dedication throughout the period. While I was still unconscious in the early days, he assured my parents, "We'll dance with him at his wedding," and indeed he accompanied me throughout the period and did not hide his excitement at every stage in the rehabilitation process. Later, an illustration of my legs appeared in a professional book on severe limb injuries written by Dr. Lerner.

I had trouble finding trousers to fit my legs. Fixed to them were metal rings of so large a diameter that I could not wear a normal pair. My Aunt Nina helped me out, finding a creative solution to the problem: she added velcro and fasteners along the sides to expand them. Her trousers allowed me to dispense with the hospital gown and helped toward my recovery.

My first actual steps since the time of injury were at Rambam, under the auspices of the dedicated Arab physiotherapist, Mahiar. I managed a few steps with a walker, my legs being supported by the metal Ilizarov splint. Dr. Lerner was, of course, present, as were my equally excited parents. I walked a few feet and the pain was intense, but my joy at walking overcame the pain. It's difficult to believe how an action so routine can suddenly lead to a moment of triumph and exaltation.

Chapter Fourteen

Orthopedic Rehabilitation

rom Rambam Hospital I was sent to the Orthopedic Rehabilitation Department at Tel Hashomer for intense physical therapy. I preferred that to the previous period, even though it meant that I had to strain and sweat, for now the amount of progress depended on my own willpower and self-discipline, whereas the previous treatment had consisted of drugs and medical treatment while I remained passive.

I woke early each morning in order to have enough time for prayers before breakfast. Then came the start of a busy schedule. I usually started by working out on my own in the physiotherapy room, the exercises changing and evolving as my condition improved. At first, most exercises were in bed, where I worked hard to strengthen the leg muscles, raising my legs repeatedly despite the weight of the metal splints. Many of my muscles not directly weakened by the injury had begun to atrophy due to prolonged inactivity in bed. Later on, I began work on the parallel bars, using various instruments to aid balance, with the Ilizarov splints taking the weight of my body, which the bone joints were still too weak to bear. The next step was physical therapy in which dedicated therapists massaged the scars on my legs and instructed me in new exercises. Thus did the hours pass until lunch. After eating, I rested a little, and then attended a study group in the synagogue. Time then to return to some arduous exercises, this time in the gymnasium, where the instructors prepared a weekly training program for me with the emphasis one day on the upper body and the next on the lower. Sometimes in the afternoon I "toured" the hospital, with a member of my family helping me to control the wheelchair. I especially enjoyed the open air outside the hospital, as I had rarely been exposed to sunlight during the winter.

Every day a group met in the hospital synagogue for *Daf Yomi*, part of a worldwide study focusing upon a different, daily page of the Talmud. Some of the participants were in wheelchairs, others attached to infusions. I joined the group and, as it took place at midday, divided my exercises into two sections. There is a special atmosphere in a group composed of people suffering from bodily ailments as they seem to rise above them, entering the world of the spirit. I too felt that the investment in study, however brief, could elevate me above the difficulties of routine treatment. Many of the students said that studying Torah helped them forget their daily troubles and pain, giving them strength to cope. Soon I was asked to act as the group's instructor, and we managed to finish Tractate Megilla close to Purim.

During my first months I traveled only by ambulance. Most of the trips were for tests at Rambam or to travel to and from home. From my early years I had loved traveling through the country and enjoying the scenery, and I had missed that during hospitalization, especially as it was so prolonged, leaving me closed inside a building, unable to see "normal places." As a result, I developed the habit on every trip of stopping at a nature spot or museum along the way, thereby visiting Naḥal Alexander, Naḥal Taninim, and Naḥal Me'arot, as well as ancient Caesarea, the fortress at the Atlit naval base, the glass museum in Kibbutz Naḥsholim, and other places. My mother accompanied me on most of these trips, and the driver kindly helped me with the wheelchair, and later with my crutches.

One day, I went with my mother and an ambulance driver to Rambam, where we met Dubi Genish who was also waiting to see Dr. Lerner. The hospital spokeswoman took the opportunity to organize an item for use in public relations, inviting photographers to take pictures of the two of us, both war-wounded, exercising in the gym under the supervision of Dr. Lerner. While we were there my mother received a phone call: "Hello, Is that Mrs. Yardenna Lubotzky? This is the security unit in Efrat."

"What's happened?" I heard my mother's worried query.

"We wish to inform you that there has been a burglary in your home."

"A burglary? Who? What did they do?"

"There were three Palestinians – but don't worry, they have all been caught." The speaker tried to calm her down.

"Three Palestinians in my house!"

It appeared that police officers, together with the community's security forces, had caught the burglars red-handed. One of them had tried to escape by sliding along the roof's gutter but was captured in the courtyard. The police handcuffed them in our house, and my younger brother Oren, a seventeen-year-old who happened to be in Efrat at the time, was summoned to act as the family representative. He contacted me with the news. I told him that the sight of caught and handcuffed men was a familiar one, but it was hard to imagine it in our living room…

The burglars had managed to overturn everything in the house, leaving an awful mess. Closets and bookshelves had been thrown down and electronic items dismantled, apparently in their search for money or valuables. However, the burglars claimed that the money in their possession belonged to them and had not been stolen from the house.

My mother and I were far from the scene, in Haifa. I realized that my mother was taking it remarkably calmly. To my surprise she said, "After what's recently happened to us, do you think I am bothered by a few burglars breaking into our house? Thank Heaven, it turned out that way. The incident could have been much more frightening if someone had been at home at the time."

Clearly, there are events in life that place everything else in perspective.

Dubi Genish had been in a ward near mine in the Department of Plastic Surgery and later in Orthopedic Rehabilitation. He was the father of three children and, when wounded, his wife Keren had been in an advanced stage of pregnancy, soon to give birth to another son. The *brit mila* had taken place at their home in Revadim and my family and I had attended the happy occasion. The dining room was crowded, as at all such events, but the atmosphere was different. The *sandak* at the *brit mila* was Uri, Dubi's colleague who had rescued him from the burning vehicle. On the completion of the ceremony, Dubi recited with emotion the blessing that ends: "…Thou who has allowed me to live and has preserved me for this day." The blessing had special significance in this instance and many of those present shed a tear. We had heard a number of stories of pregnant wives who, when giving birth a few months later, had embraced the newborn as widows. Dubi had been blessed to join his family in introducing the child into the covenant of Abraham.

One day I learned that there was a new patient in the Respiratory Rehabilitation Department: Rafael Gerstein, father of Brigadier General Erez Gerstein. As a soldier in the IDF and, in particular, as a member of the Golani, I had grown up with the myth of that revered officer killed in Lebanon in 1999 when he was commander of the Lebanon Liaison Unit. Erez had become one of the most admired symbols of the Golani Brigade, and had fulfilled many significant roles, finally becoming brigade commander. The legends woven around him and the admiration demonstrated by our officers (who had been his subordinates) had transformed him into a model for all officers in the Golani Brigade. I went to visit Rafael, where I met Shula, his wife, feeding him. Rafael could not speak, due to the breathing tube that had been inserted, but communicated by writing on a whiteboard. I told Shula and Rafael that, though I had never met their son in person, the loss was still felt in the army, with stories of him often related in evening sessions devoted to education or geography. I personally had also, when speaking to soldiers about love of one's country, recounted stories of the life and death of Erez Gerstein as a committed patriot, and an outstanding commander and educator. Shula could not hide her excitement and Rafael wrote me a warm message. In subsequent visits, I brought to Rafael's ward the soldiers who came to visit me, thinking that the sight of soldiers in uniform with the beret and insignia of the Golani Brigade who cherish the memory of Erez Gerstein would make the couple happy. The soldiers, too, were excited to meet the parents of the mythical general, having heard so much about him. Rafael had apparently suffered from a broken heart when his son died and, a few weeks after being hospitalized, his heart failed him. On the eighth anniversary of Erez's death, Rafael died and was buried in the cemetery at Reshafim, beside his son.

During the rehabilitation period, I became very sensitive to the problem of accessibility, of physical access for the disabled and their wheelchairs. Suddenly everything required advanced planning, checking that the place was reachable. I had no choice but to visit many buildings that were not wheelchair-accessible, and that very much troubled me. I could not reach the homes of many of my friends if the entrance was via a number of stairs, and did not like to have people carry me up in the wheelchair unless there was a special need. Once, at the end of Shabbat, I went with others to visit a friend in Jerusalem, having checked in advance that there was an elevator in the building, but when we arrived it turned out to my dismay that the elevator had broken down, so that I was unable to go up to his apartment.

When I started to walk with crutches new possibilities opened up, but the problem of accessibility for the disabled continued to trouble me. I tried and am continuing to try to raise public awareness of this problem. It infuriates me to see businesses or public buildings that are inaccessible, or even coffee houses that are built one step above the street. I found myself often complaining to the managers there but I never received a satisfactory answer why I should be prohibited from using the place. I was very pleased to see the work of the Ma'aglei Tzedek "Paths of Righteousness" movement on this topic.

The IDF's Medical Corps held a ceremony at Beit Haḥayal in Tel Aviv to mark the end of the Second Lebanon War. I was invited to tell the story of my injury and to describe the medical treatment I had received. To my great pleasure, I met there the medical team that had treated me during my injury. They told me about the moments of tension when they reached the border, with firing continuing non-stop, and the urgency of transferring me to the helicopter. On seeing the severe condition of my legs, they decided, they said, to salvage what they could. The right leg looked obviously ready for amputation. They applied the tourniquet below the knee to mark the lowest point of amputation, imagining that they would thus save at least the knee joint. They were amazed to see that, in the end, my leg had not been amputated. After exchanging experiences, I was called to go on stage, to describe the injuries and to report on my present medical condition. After my talk, Dr. Oren Ben-Lulu came on stage, one of the doctors who had treated me in the field. He first recounted the rescue from the Lebanese border, and then suggested that my medical case should become a subject for study by the Medical Corps from which to draw lessons.

The main topic was the problem of tourniquets. In many instances, a tourniquet obviously saves lives, as, in massive bleeding, the patient might die from loss of blood, and the tourniquet can stop the bleeding. But in many cases it can cause severe damage to the limb, leading to amputation. Damage is particularly severe when the rescue takes many hours, and the blood flow is blocked for a long period. It is very difficult to decide whether the injury requires a tourniquet or whether it is better to avoid using it in order not to damage the limb. Sometimes, in the heat of battle, and under great pressure in dealing with numerous victims, it is preferable to use a tourniquet. It is a simple and swift solution to the problem of bleeding. But, as mentioned, there is a risk in such treatment. Ultimately, the decision to use a tourniquet and the duration depends on the medic in the field. It may be a fateful decision. In my case, the doctors decided to remove the tourniquet from my left leg, and for the right leg to replace it lower down, below the knee. Those decisions proved successful: they were able to save my leg from being amputated and yet stem the loss of blood. Again, I learned that the decisions made in real time by a clever and sensitive team, with the help of Providence, eventually saved me.

In the hospital, and perhaps even more during the period of rehabilitation, my family and I came to know some wonderful volunteers of various ages who had decided to contribute their strength and energy to help and cheer wounded soldiers. They assisted in every way possible, organizing many events, birthdays parties in restaurants and performances by artists at the rehabilitation center. Every week we had numerous visitors, often bringing gourmet meals and original gifts. They arranged for tickets to ball games and concerts in accordance with the interests of the soldiers. It revealed a wonderful aspect of Israel, volunteerism, the desire to help others. They helped us get through difficult times and eased matters for our families. They made sure that each patient had a refrigerator in his room and a microwave if needed. On certain weekdays we knew in advance that we should not eat too much at dinner, for at night there arrived tasty, home-cooked meals or bought food. There was also a wheelchair table tennis club, with a former youth champion to assist.

Every few weeks we went to a restaurant to celebrate a birthday party or a person's release from the rehabilitation center. It was a complicated logistical operation to move us all to the restaurant in vehicles large enough for our wheelchairs. The honoree of these parties received, in addition to other gifts, a large picture of himself. I received the picture of me laying *tefillin* after the battle in Bint Jbeil. The pictures were often accompanied by humorous images, such as a car bumper sticker with the words: "Disabled, but ahead of you!"

The rehabilitation period created warm friendships between me and the many wounded from the war. We held long talks on our experiences in the war and its aftermath, in-depth discussions on our wounds and their treatment, all of which created a unique comradeship between us. Often we found that we had been in the same battle without having met each other. Every patient was interested in his friend's condition, and supported him at difficult moments. Sometimes it is easier to share one's experiences and emotions with someone who has undergone the same. In addition, the long stay together in the same place created a sense of brotherhood.

In the rehabilitation center, I shared a room with Gidon Goldenberg, a deputy company commander from the Golani's Orev anti-tank unit, who was wounded by a missile fired by the Air Force in Bint Jbeil. We discovered that Gete had been involved in rescuing him, and so another connection was made. Our room became the focus of visits from members of the Golani Brigade, its flags being hung proudly on the walls. We passed the time with a sense of humor and a positive attitude to life, and Gidon always had us rolling in laughter at his witty jokes. He succeeded in softening the seriousness and worry of the wounded around him, encouraging them to see their situation more optimistically, even humorously. We coined expressions and phrases that an outsider would not have understood, and Gidon even began writing "A Complete Dictionary for Those Who Are Not…"

As already mentioned, Gidon was wounded by fire from an Air Force plane directed by Egoz and that formed the basis for a few interesting situations. When the chief of staff, Dan Halutz, came to the rehabilitation center to visit those wounded in the war, Gidon asked him: "Do you know what Mahmoud Abu Hanoud and I have in common?" In response to Halutz's surprised look, Gidon replied, "We were both wounded by the Israel Air Force…"

Some time later, an Air Force officer paid a visit and asked, "Which one is Gidon?" When he saw Gidon lying wounded in bed, he lowered his gaze. Then he raised his head and identified himself as the pilot who had fired the missile that hit Gidon. Gidon smiled and eased the tension in the room. The pilot related the incident from his perspective. He said he could not see which forces were in the building. He simply identified on the map the building he had to target and fired. The pilot's remorse, as in other cases of friendly fire, can be very difficult to bear. Gidon tried his utmost to relieve him, expressing no anger, and turning the whole situation into a joke. He added that, during the incident, the commander of Orev had requested Air Force assistance but was informed that they were busy helping Egoz and would turn to them as soon as they had finished…

Gidon was determined to return to the army, and trained hard to achieve his goal. Two years later, Gidon returned to the army as company commander of the Fifty-First Battalion recruits.

One day soldiers from my company came to visit me and the conversation turned to the battalion's heavy loss of equipment during the war. From the conversation, it emerged that in my charred flak jacket (which was hit by the missile) was not only my fighting equipment, but all of the company's missing equipment…

Acts of mischief and humor were the province not only of the newly wounded soldiers. In the rehabilitation center there was also a group of veterans from earlier wars in Israel returning for hospitalization. They used to tease each other at night, for example by stealthily swapping their friends' prostheses, which were recovered in the morning to the sound of shrieks of laughter. It was an amusing sight to see them form a train of wheelchairs with, at the head, Micah with a Moshe Dayan patch over one eye from a wound in the Yom Kippur War, seated on a motorized wheelchair, and behind him a column of friends each holding onto the headrest of the wheelchair in front. Micah also used to wear a bandana on his head to look like a one-eyed pirate. One person described the scene as "the body crying and the soul laughing." It was obvious that they had created a special bond. Just as in a reserve unit soldiers get together every year, so this group met regularly at the hospital or in rehabilitation. Every morning they used to make a well-seasoned salad, rich in vegetables, and share it with the other patients and medical professionals. We younger patients fitted in well with them and the contact between the generations was an inexhaustible source of jokes and laughter. We, the newly wounded, were the young children of the "family" of the injured.

As during the early period of hospitalization, so at the beginning of the rehabilitation process many injured veterans came to visit me and helped me understand what I was to expect. They organized jeep tours in which they included the newly wounded, beautifully organized trips, to stunning locations, with excellent guides and good food. Beyond the great pleasure those trips gave me, the organizers had another purpose. They wanted to show us how to overcome a serious injury, how to deal with the difficulties, and how to live a full and enjoyable life. In talks along the way, they told us about the long rehabilitation process, prepared us for the future, and strengthened our spirits. In those meetings, we met people with complex physical disabilities, but with a fresh and healthy approach to life.

During my rehabilitation, new casualties arrived from Gaza and the West Bank. I, who was a veteran compared to them, visited them in their hospital wards and tried to encourage them as the veterans had encouraged me. I talked a lot with their families. My parents often accompanied me on these visits, contributing their experience as parents of the injured. Those visits encouraged us too, reminding us how far I had progressed despite the early problems.

Many emotions follow an injury, not always possible to identify or characterize. I met numerous injured people, not only soldiers, who responded in various ways. Many felt frustrated, realizing that they would never be as they once were. Others felt angry, sometimes angry in general and sometimes directing their anger at the source responsible for the injury. There are those who come to terms with the situation with a determination to move ahead, or through apathy. And the same person can change from time to time. In the words of Ecclesiastes: "There is a time to slay and a time to heal…a time to weep and a time to laugh…a time to be silent and a time to speak, a time to love and a time to hate, a time for war and a time for peace."

Sometimes emotions are mixed. A basic feeling that had accompanied me from the time of the injury was a sense of gratitude. I knew the suffering that the injury had caused me and those around me. Nevertheless, I felt that I had much to be thankful for. The comparison prominent in my mind was with those of my friends who had not returned. To me, all pains and difficulties were dwarfed by the suffering of the bereaved families. Such consciousness is hard to live with, but perhaps my direct encounters with the dead had left their mark.

A few days after Ḥanukkah, more than four months after the injury, we received an invitation to an evening in honor of wounded infantrymen. It was an impressive annual ceremony, devoted this year mainly to those wounded in the Second Lebanon War. Invitations were sent to the war wounded, stating that the event would be honored by the presence of senior members of the defense establishment, including army generals, the chief of staff, and the defense minister. In the months since the war ended, public criticism had mounted against the leaders responsible for directing it. Leading the charge were reservists and representatives of the bereaved families, but the wounded also had something to say. In my ward, a number of seriously injured were furious, saying, "They invite us to an evening in our honor and bring the people who caused the failure to honor us? Celebrating, as if we won the war."

"Who said we didn't win? That's only the talk of the post-modernist media designed to confuse us. We hit the Ḥezbollah hard. Intelligence claims hundreds of terrorists are dead and there's severe damage to the infrastructure. We destroyed their posts, captured ammunition dumps, and made them retreat from the border posts."

"What are you talking about? An army with superior techno-logy, total control of the air, tanks and tens of thousands of soldiers assigned to the campaign against what? – a small guerrilla organiza-tion. We should have crushed them. The IDF was prepared to fight on several fronts with entire armies. Here the whole campaign was in one sector against a few thousand terrorists." The speaker argued passionately and many around him nodded in agreement.

Another patient joined in: "We had the ability to win, but the orders were confused; there was a lack of professionalism. The root of the problem was at the higher echelons and reached down to the local commanders. There was a failure to reach the target and fulfill the mission at all costs. That's not the way to fight."

"But those in the actual battle fought like lions. Maybe there were mistakes in the command, but in the actual battles we defeated the terrorists."

Some justified the decision to go to war: "It was a just war, and in war there are casualties. Would it have been better to hold back? To allow Ḥezbollah forces to continue to arm for battle? Should Ḥezbollah be allowed to attack an IDF patrol on our territory, kill sol-diers, and abduct two without having to bear the consequences?"

"They thought we could finish the affair by aerial bombard-ment. You can't defeat a guerrilla organization without seeing the whites of their eyes. We should have begun by entering the terrain and clearing the whole area up to the Litani River."

One of the wounded broke in: "Clear the area? Do you know how many casualties we would have suffered that way? Hezbollah was only waiting for that. We should have bombed from the air and then immediately called for a cease-fire – gain politically without having to pay the price in blood."

They began giving examples from the battles in which they had participated. Each story reflected a different aspect of the war in Lebanon. Strategic and tactical arguments mingled with diplomatic and political. Some of the injured were entrenched in their positions while others were persuaded by the arguments of others. These discussions were not, of course, without parallel but their uniqueness lay in the fact that they came from people who had fought personally in the battle and, more importantly, had paid a heavy price – with their bodies.

The sense of frustration was greatest among those who felt that their injuries had been unnecessary. I listened to the debate, very interested in the war and its results. As a citizen, I was worried about the army's degree of success and the lessons to be learned from the war. I was also interested in the part my own unit had played in it, but did not feel any special emotional involvement because of my injury. While it was true that I was one of the many who had paid a heavy personal price, the price was not unbearable, at least to me. Bereavement is a heavier price, bar none, compared to any form of personal injury. During the war itself, I had been unaware of any public criticism, partly because it only arose later and partly because I was not greatly exposed to the media. Only after the war did I learn of the public's frustration and was able to develop my own views; but during fighting, such criticism or the drawing of conclusions did not concern me. The war had broken out in response to the kidnapping of soldiers by Hezbollah, and the State of Israel had responded to the violation of its sovereignty. For me, as a fighter and as a commander participating in the fighting, there were tasks to be carried out. I received orders at the tactical level. Conducting attacks and entering villages seemed logical tasks in combat against the enemy. Were those orders emanating from higher command wrong? For a platoon commander in time of warfare, the question is irrelevant.

Even the frequent changes of orders were seen by many as a necessity of war. For us this was our first war, and we had no others with which to compare it.

One day in February 2007, when my legs were still in metal splints, I went for a trip in the North together with my friend Ariel Gino from Egoz, who had taken a sniper bullet in his jaw at Bint Jbeil, and with Jonathan from the Twelfth Battalion. Each of us had fought in the Golani Brigade but in different areas of Lebanon. The trip, which we called "Following the Path of the Fighters," was to visit the places on the Israeli border from which we had watched the battle zones. We began the tour at the site of the kidnapping near Zar'it. We drove along the road near the border fence, entering bases along the border.

The soldiers in the guard posts could not refuse our request to enter, and not only because of the officer certificates we presented. It was our request as wounded veterans of the last war that counted. We entered the observation post and war room, and from there recognized our route, the various buildings we had passed, and the Pagoda on the ridge near Maroun A-Ras. Ariel also identified the hole in the wall made by a missile at Maroun A-Ras in a battle in which he had participated and in which five soldiers from Egoz had been killed. The men in the war room agreed to show us videos from the war. We passed by my last point of entry to Lebanon, near Malkia, and identified the place where I was wounded. As we returned to the observation point, I remembered my own decision to return there. I saw a few road signs for armored vehicles that had not yet been fixed and I identified places marked by the fires that had burned there during the war. All in all, however, the northern region had blossomed once again. How happy I was to go there, even if only in a vehicle, visiting the hiking trails and dirt roads. Israelis and tourists, individuals and families, were again traveling on the northern roads. At Avivim, I saw a woman pushing a stroller, and the streets of the towns were filled with boys and girls at play. Another circle had closed.

One day, Ran from the psychological staff of the hospital called me. He said that as part of his studies he was conducting research on those wounded in the war. Normally I do not like filling in psychological questionnaires, but I knew that Ran himself had been wounded in Lebanon a few years earlier (in fact he was known as "the last casualty in Lebanon before the withdrawal"), and decided to grant his request. I received a large envelope filled with the pages of the questionnaire. I had to answer many questions, mostly multiple-choice. I answered them quickly, but I stopped at the question: "At what point in your life could you have acted differently in order to avoid the injury?"

I stared at the page. Strange that so far this question had not preoccupied me. Where to begin? Better to start from the end and go backward. I began to write:

Had I not stood up, but continued to sit when the missile struck. In fact, had I been sitting, I would not be answering the questionnaire today.

Had I moved to another position in the column of vehicles. I probably would not have been wounded, but someone else would have been wounded instead.

Had I not left on the mission, one of the company's commanders would have had to replace me.

Had I refused to go on the mission for fear of being attacked during daylight.

Had I not registered for officer training.

Had I not joined Golani but another brigade.

I stopped at the end of the page. There were so many scenarios that could possibly have prevented the injury, but the truth is that most of them had never occurred to me until I was faced with the questionnaire. First, as a believer, I accept the concept of divine decree, but even without becoming involved in theology, my view is that the ways of the Lord are wonderful and we are not to challenge them. Yet there was another point that bothered me in this discussion. There are intersections in life when one is faced with a decision. How to choose? One must consider carefully the various arguments and strive to be honest with oneself and at peace with the decision. But one can only consider the possibilities that are visible. "A judge can only see what is before him." The possibilities being considered may be faulty. The result reflects the correct decision only if it is a direct continuation of the decision, otherwise it cannot be included in the considerations of the individual. If the decision was based on moral motives and stood the test of common sense, it was, to my way of thinking, the right decision, even if it led to an unfortunate result.

I looked at the page I had filled out. I remember there was just one place where I could not decide how to answer. Should I have joined an officers' training course? It was after I had accidentally hurt my hand, suffering a cut that tore three tendons and severely limited its mobility. I had been summoned to a committee to determine my military profile and it was decided that it was too low to permit combat service and certainly prohibited acceptance into an Infantry Officers' Course. After six months of rehabilitation, physical therapy, and occupational therapy, I filed an appeal and requested a reassessment from the medical board. Equipped with the appropriate documents and motivation, I managed to raise the profile. There was an orthopedic reservation but it did not prevent me from attending the course. However, I still suffered some limitations in my right hand. For this and other reasons, I debated whether to take the course. On looking back, I do not think my injury influenced my decision fundamentally. There are risks everywhere in life, and the risks in military service have an ethical aspect: the defense of Israel and the homeland.

The head of the Orthopedic Rehabilitation Department at Tel Hashomer is Dr. Itzhak Siev-Ner. It turned out that our families had a shared past: the mother of Dr. Siev-Ner was a friend of my grandfather, Iser Lubotzky. They had fought together as partisans in the forests of Lithuania. My grandfather came to visit me in rehabilitation and met Dr. Siev-Ner whom he had known as a child. My grandfather was full of stories about that earlier time and his experiences with Anna, Siev-Ner's mother. It included a surprising story. In one of the fights against the Nazis, he was hit in the leg by a bullet and was evacuated to one the bases in the forest. Medical treatment was minimal, with almost no bandages. The nurse bandaged his wounds with bandages made of tree leaves. The wound became infected and my grandfather got a high fever. Partisans captured a German drug delivery, and were able to give my grandfather an antibiotic, prontosil.

The fever decreased and he finally recovered from his injuries. The nurse who had cared for my grandfather was none other than Anna Azgud (later Siev-Ner). History repeats itself, and over sixty years later, her son, a doctor, was treating my legs.

During the conversation, I noticed that my grandfather often spoke of "the war" without mentioning which. He of course meant World War II. It seems that in every generation there is a war to which everyone refers. During the past decades, there had been two world wars, and in the early days of the State of Israel, no doubt everyone referred to the War of Independence. In my parents' generation, it was the Yom Kippur War. For my generation, it will remain the Second Lebanon War.

Chapter Fifteen

The Return Home

I was released from the rehabilitation center about seven-and-a-half months after my injury. For the next few months, I continued to receive treatment at Tel Hashomer and to combine them with study at the Ma'ale Adumim yeshiva in which I had been studying before entering the army. At the yeshiva, a festive meal was held in thanksgiving that all its students had returned safely from the war. Although I had been injured, by divine grace I had returned to normal life. All students were invited to the impressive event, held on a Saturday night, together with alumni and their families. The ceremony was conducted by Rabbi Sabato. The Rosh Yeshiva, Rabbi Rabinovitch, who spoke to the gathering, and then students who had participated in the war told of their ordeals and described the many miracles they had experienced during the fighting. One of them related how a grenade had been hurled at the soldiers but failed to explode.

Finally, my father and mother spoke, followed by me. During the evening, videos of the war were shown, accompanied by music, with expressions of gratitude offered to Heaven. Afterward, a number of people came over to me to say, with tears in their eyes, how deeply they had been moved by the ceremony. They felt connected to the events and before returning to their normal lives, recalled their own experiences of life and death.

Three months later I had further surgery at Rambam. This time, Dr. Lerner removed the splints from my right leg, after which I was hospitalized for four weeks, again in the Orthopedic Rehabilitation Department at Tel Hashomer. I was assigned a room next to the one I had before. Everything was so familiar and yet so strange. I already knew the place, the procedures, and the medical staff, though, of course, the patients had changed. It was difficult to return, as I had regarded that period as closed, so this time I wanted it to be only temporary. I brought minimum equipment from home, hung no Golani flags on the walls, and concentrated on the physical therapy.

During treatment, I was exposed to the most advanced and up-to-date medical practices. The very thought of grafting a muscle onto a leg and extending its length was exciting. My interest in the field increased. Beyond wanting to understand the treatment I was undergoing, I tried to grasp certain principles of medicine, talking a lot with the medical staff and learning about their techniques. I began to experience a desire to study medicine, feeling that it would be a mission, a real way to help people, to improve their physical and mental conditions and to ease their pain. I also believed that my own experience would allow me to understand the patients' feelings. The field had interested me even before the injury, but I doubt whether I would have decided to study medicine without it. That injury changed the course of my life; I registered at the Faculty of Medicine at the Hebrew University in Jerusalem for the coming school year. My brother-in-law, Maru Gete, who had been attracted to the profession before me, registered for medicine at Ben-Gurion University in Be'er Sheva.

A year had passed since the Second Lebanon War, and it was time to hold memorial services for the fallen. Each family set the date for the memorial. However, even though eight soldiers had been killed at Bint Jbeil on the same day, the services were held on different days and at different times. Some fixed the anniversary according to the date of death, others according to the date of burial. Moreover, not all had been buried the same day; some were buried after sunset which counts in Jewish tradition as the next day. One family had delayed the burial until the mother arrived from overseas. Some went according to the Gregorian date and not the Hebrew, so that the services were spread over an entire week and a half. I managed to attend almost all of them, together with Alon Hakima, who had been the commander of Company C in the battle and had been seriously wounded by grenade shrapnel and bullets in his abdomen and pelvis, yet had managed since then to return to army service. He drove me to the cemeteries in his car, and sometimes even to the families' homes.

Apart from Roi Klein, all the fallen had been soldiers and commanders from Alon's company. It was not easy to return to those memories and hard times. I discussed with Alon the feeling that our injuries had made it easier for us to talk with the bereaved parents, as sometimes those who survive a battle are left with a sense of guilt. An officer's injury is a kind of proof that he did everything he could to protect his soldiers, almost losing his life in the process.

A video to the memory of Roi Klein repeatedly played the song "*Ana Beko'ach*" by Ovadia Hamama, an Israeli singer made famous by that song, and it was played at many other memorials. Alon asked me about the origin of the song and where he could obtain a copy. I told him it was from a poem by the Tanna R. Nehunia b. Hakana, which is often recited on Friday night. I did not know where to buy the song, but later contacted Hamama. When he heard the background, he was thrilled and surprised Alon by sending him the disc with a warm dedication.

The Golani Casualties Department organized a day tour in the North for the bereaved families of the battalion, together with the wounded. Early in the morning, we drove north, Maru, my brother-in-law, accompanying me. We stopped in the forest to see the place where the battalion had prepared for its first entry into Lebanon. Then we approached the security fence near Avivim, where it had crossed the border on its way to Bint Jbeil. The next stop was at the outpost Rakefet overlooking the combat zone during the war.

Asor, who had been the commander of the Fifty-First Battalion during the war, outlined the main events and pointed out to the participants the Muslim domes and villages that were visible from the observation post. Those of us who knew the area and were familiar with the map explained the battalion's movements to the families. The day concluded with a ceremony at the Birya forest, where a camping ground, previously known as "The Twist," was renamed "The Brothers' Recreation Area," in memory of the ten soldiers from the Fifty-First Battalion who had fallen there in the Second Lebanon War. The rededication was initiated by the Keren Kayemet in cooperation with the "Golani Faithful" organization, the project being the idea of Avichay Yaakov, who had been a squad commander in Riflemen C during the war.

During the summer, our family celebrated my father's birthday in a restaurant at Gush Etzion. Nearby sat a group of my father's friends and in the course of conversation it turned out that one of their sons was in the Golani. They called me over to talk to him and I recognized him. It was Roi Levy, operations officer of the Golani Brigade during the war. At that time, he was the company commander of the Orev Unit of the Golani and was about to be reassigned to command the Reconnaissance Unit. Roi asked in which battle I had been wounded, and I recounted the sequence of events as far as I knew it. He listened calmly and said he had something to add: "It was I who sent you on that mission," and he proceeded to tell me of the events from his point of view. He remembered the debate whether to send us out or postpone, and explained his decision, the logistic need to open the route for the forces in the field. I told him that I bore him no grudge. Everyone needs to act according to his understanding. I was glad to hear further details from him and we parted as friends.

The Fifty-First Battalion was now in action in the southern Gaza Strip, engaging in numerous missions. In one of the operations on October 17, 2007, a unit from Riflemen A engaged a group of Hamas terrorists, and in the course of the assault Sergeant Ben Kubani was hit and killed. His funeral was held the next day in the military cemetery in Ḥadera. He had been a member of Maru Gete's platoon. After the funeral I went with Maru to visit his family, yet another scene of bereavement that seemed to return us to the days of funerals and memorial services of the previous year. But we knew that the battle-scarred Fifty-First Battalion would stand firm and continue to fulfill its tasks. In another operation two months later, when a unit of the Third Rifles engaged terrorists, the men came under fire in the house where they were staying, and returned fire. One soldier, Gabi Ziv, was hit in the arm and leg, and during the rescue mission the building was hit by a missile, the explosion injuring several fighters. Gabi was wounded again, this time with a serious head injury. He was evacuated by helicopter to Soroka Hospital in Be'er Sheva.

Gabi had been a soldier in my platoon. The following day, I visited the intensive care unit at Soroka, where he was unconscious, with no clear diagnosis of the extent of the damage to his head. I met Gabi's worried family. They remembered me from ceremonies in the past. I told them again how, when I was his commander, he had been injured in Gaza when his armored vehicle overturned. Then I mentioned how he had just missed being hurt when a closet fell on his head as a result of an explosion in the village of Maḥibab in Lebanon. But the family was especially thrilled to hear that he had been one of the soldiers who carried me on a stretcher from our vehicle to the rescue tank after my injury. I added that I felt it my duty to come and support them in this difficult time, first as his past commander, but particularly as he had helped me in my hour of need. After several nerve-wracking weeks, Gabi awoke and began a long rehabilitation process at the Lowenstein Center in Ra'anana, where he managed to surprise his doctors by the speed of his progress.

I was released from the Outpatients Department at Tel Hashomer and began receiving treatment every day at Beit Haloḥem in Jerusalem. On Shabbat prior to beginning studies at the university (which had been postponed because of a lengthy strike there) my family held a thanksgiving celebration in Efrat. Dr. Alex Lerner and his wife Galia were our guests for Shabbat, together with Achikam Halpern who had been a platoon commander with me in the same company, and had pulled me out of the vehicle after I was wounded. Achikam had continued to serve in the army and, coming from Gaza, only barely managed to reach us before Shabbat.

On Friday, my father took the Lerners on a tour of the museums in Kfar Etzion and Herodion. During the Friday night service, Rabbi Shlomo Riskin, the rabbi of Efrat, devoted his sermon to the importance of saving life and of a doctor's work, concluding by welcoming the two guests. Dr. Lerner was happy to hear the rabbi mention Maimonides, the "Rambam," after whom the hospital at which he worked was named. He invited me to come to specialize in orthopedics at Rambam when I finished my medical studies.

At the Shabbat meal, Achikam reviewed the details of the battle, from the time of the initial encounter to the end of the rescue operation, and Dr. Lerner continued with the details of the night I reached the hospital. It was after a period of forty-eight hours when he had worked continuously treating numerous casualties from Lebanon. He said that at first sight it was clear the doctors would have to amputate my right leg, but after a careful examination and the fact that my left leg was also badly damaged, he decided to try to save the right leg. He also explained that his decisions concerning whether to use the Ilizarov method depend not only on the state of the injury, but also on the character of the casualty. The leg extension process is difficult and tedious, but it also requires great responsibility on the part of the patient as the screws have to be turned at the appointed time without missing even a single rotation, and also the leg must be kept clean, particularly where the screws are inserted. Dr. Lerner added jokingly that at first he thought I was an Ethiopian because of my charred and blackened skin.

On Shabbat morning, after prayers, we held a Kiddush for the residents of Efrat. Friends of the local residents and people who happened to be visiting Efrat also joined in. Dozens of people crowded together and Dr. Lerner addressed them, talking about the war and his first acquaintance with me, and concluded by saying how thrilled he was by Zionism and his love of the country to which he had immigrated. After that, I was called on to say a few words. I referred to the concept of challenges in Judaism, quoting from the weekly Torah portion, *Vayera*, which tells of the Binding of Isaac. I talked about insights and thoughts that came after the war. My family and I thanked Dr. Lerner and Achikam, the Efrat residents, and my friends for their support, with a special thanks to Heaven for having saved me. That Shabbat was a milestone for me. Until then, I had been a patient undergoing treatment; but from then onward I became a person living out his life, a student at university, even though I would still need to go for treatment from time to time.

Afterword

After the Battle

War and injury involve much pain and suffering, but
they are also unique experiences from which lessons can be learned
and by which one can mature. First, they provide a sense of proportion concerning many things in life. Worries and concerns to which
people attribute great importance grow pale and less significant in
the face of death and physical injury, the moments when a person
must struggle with powerful life forces. Priorities change, fundamental
issues find their place at the top of the ladder, and small, materialistic
issues slide to the bottom.

Such moments require us to overcome our weaknesses, to
discover the power of faith, and to grow spiritually. The sense of gratitude toward the Creator increases, achieving a more stable dimension. Prayers recited routinely receive new meaning. For example,
the morning prayers begin with blessing the Creator who "makes
the blind to see," with its relevance to wounded soldiers who have
lost their sight; "who frees the bound" – our friends taken hostage or
still missing; "who places the land on the water" – allowing the lame
to walk once again on solid ground; and of course the blessing from

the prayers a little later: "who provides a long and speedy recovery for all our ills." I was especially moved by that wonderful verse from Psalm 116: "You have saved my soul from death, my eyes from weeping, and my legs from collapsing." Recognizing that the injury was not in vain can itself be a source of strength. We went out to protect our fellow citizens who were huddled in shelters in the North. We fought in a Jewish army guarding Israel on the principle that "Jewish blood can no longer be ignored"; we attacked those who rose against us and we were wounded while holding weapons in our hands. On gazing back at the history of the Jewish people, that fact has great significance. My grandfather fought heroically as a partisan against the Nazis and, when pursued and wounded, hid in the forest, constantly on the run. We went into battle, protecting the Jewish State in the Land of Israel.

Throughout the recovery period I had support and warm affection from many sources. There were the groups of volunteers, wonderful people who gave their time and energy to assist the war wounded, either within an organization or independently. In general, during the war and subsequent to it, there was a real sense of unity among the people, and the desire of ordinary individuals to help and support anyone they could.

During rehabilitation I met many casualties, old and young. I met people who had the spiritual strength to live their lives fully, despite their disabilities. Through conversations with them I learned much about resilience and how to overcome a loss. The recovery process and the struggle for life affect not only one's mental strength, but also one's sensitivity to the suffering of others. In *Man's Search for Meaning*, Viktor Frankl argued that difficult or traumatic events can trigger such a search.

In brief, suffering an injury can contribute much to a person's character. Suffering an injury is not to be recommended – I would not wish anyone to experience it; but once it has occurred it can be a formative experience, an experience to accompany one throughout one's life. Optimism is a conscious decision to integrate into normal life, to be thankful for what we have, and to move forward with confidence.

Today, two years after my injury, I can remember all that occurred, but with the ability to look forward. Compared to the situation before being wounded, my physical condition is, of course, worse; but it is possible to draw honey from the sting. The challenges I was compelled to face strengthened my spirit and endowed me with a broader and deeper understanding. Concluding this book marks the closing of a circle and the opening of a new chapter in my life.

A Letter to My Platoon

I wrote this a few weeks after my injury:

Dear Members of the Third Platoon,

   I would have liked to talk to the members of our platoon face to face, with all of us in the same room, but as circumstances do not permit that, I shall resort instead to writing you a letter.

   Let me begin with some dry facts. After a few weeks' fighting in Lebanon, we were granted a period of recreation and were then moved to Malkia as a reserve brigade unit. On Wednesday, August 9, 2006, we received orders to supply water, food, medical equipment, maps, and other items to the brigade's battalions in Bint Jbeil. We left in the afternoon from report line 252 in a mounted column of tanks and armored vehicles. My vehicle contained a crew of three: Ori the driver, Ohad the gunner, and myself as commander. We were third in line, with the lead tank ahead and Gal, the company commander, in the next vehicle. We had traveled for two and a half kilometers when I suddenly saw a distant flash. Immediately after, an anti-tank missile struck our vehicle. It hit exactly the commander's section, but at that moment, instead of being seated there, I was standing on the seat with the hatch open, so that it hit the lower part of my body, but missed the upper. Ori, who was in the driver's seat, reported that he was fine, and Ohad announced that he was somewhat dazed but functioning. I tried unsuccessfully to make radio contact, but Achikam who was traveling in the vehicle behind, soon came up together with the Company Rescue Unit. They extricated us swiftly and efficiently. At first, they tried to open the rear elevator and evacuate us through it, but the vehicle was full of equipment, so I shouted to them that it would be better to take us through the upper deck. We were taken to the upper deck and from there evacuated by tank together with a medic, with Ohad in the company commander's vehicle, while Ori traveled in another. We reached the border, where a trained medical team awaited us, providing initial treatment of our wounds. We were then transferred to a helicopter that flew us directly to Rambam Hospital. I was fully conscious throughout the journey. Further details you can no doubt obtain from the soldiers.

Ohad was found to have burns on his face, to have suffered from some shrapnel and was defined as in fair condition. Ori was lightly wounded, having broken a finger. Both were transferred to Soroka Hospital in Be'er Sheva and released a few days later. I was classed as "seriously injured" with the possibility of having my right leg amputated and with an open fracture in my left leg, shrapnel in my body, burns on face and hands and, of course, loss of blood. I underwent an immediate operation, was sedated, and placed in intensive care. I awoke on Friday night to find my family around my bed reciting the prayers for Erev Shabbat. Their joy was indescribable and I too had a comforting surprise: having seen the condition of my right leg during the rescue, I was convinced it had been amputated, yet discovered that the surgeons had decided to attempt to save it.

I will not bore you with the medical details, but in general I am due to undergo a series of orthopedic and plastic surgery to save the leg, and then switch to rehabilitation, with the goal being that at the end of the process I will stand on both feet. The road ahead is still very long and full of difficulties, but I believe I am moving in the right direction.

That is a brief summary of the situation, but it seems to me more important to discuss the meaning of it all. Throughout the course, we talked a great deal about the significance of being a fighter, understanding the value of friendship, of protecting the country, of loving and preserving it. Many values may seem vague and hazy during training, but suddenly, when we are called to battle, these values are given renewed life and meaning.

Throughout my time as platoon commander, I tried to inculcate in the platoon a love for our country, through geographical surveys, recounting events that occurred in various locations, through nature expeditions, descriptions of landscapes, and so forth. I believe that there are three main ways to learn to love one's country. One is studying maps, identifying every town, wadi, and mountain; in that way connecting with places and feeling one belongs to them. The second method is to experience it physically, to walk through it on foot, to visit sites, hills, and rivers, enjoying the country by having it unfold before one's eyes.

There is, however, a third way; namely, fighting on its soil. Fighting for it and paying a price in blood makes us part of it. A person who goes into battle for his country, who soaks the ground with his sweat, even with his blood, will love the country. He will feel that it is his own, that he is inextricably linked to it.

We did not choose to go to war. Although we are fighters, we are not aggressors eager for battle. Yet, when the time comes, we know very well why we fight. We are fighting for the people of Israel, in order to protect the country's citizens and to defend them. "Be strong and be strengthened for our people, and for the cities of our Lord," the Torah informs us. That is not just rhetoric. We set out for the Second Lebanon War at a time when the residents in the North were living under constant shelling. We were not prompted by feelings of militancy, but of solidarity with our fellow citizens sitting in shelters in the North. Our aim was to bring quiet and security to Northern Israel. During the fighting, an unparalleled friendship was formed between us, making us "brothers in arms" in the fullest sense. We found in each other wonderful qualities, including a willingness to risk our lives for each other.

War demands a heavy price and we have indeed paid a heavy personal price; but we went to war with a clear purpose and a readiness to absorb these losses. We knew very well that we might pay with our lives or with bodily injury, but we realized we were sent to protect the northern communities. Here, incidentally, is the connection that I talked about earlier, the connection to Israel. We saw communities deserted, some of them partially destroyed, creating in us a strong desire to return to see those places blooming and prospering.

I personally have also paid a price, but I thank Heaven for the grace bestowed on me and my family. There is no point in speculating "what if," as sufficient miracles have been granted me: my head is undamaged, my mind is clear and functioning, my upper body is whole. Although I have to undergo a long and by no means simple rehabilitation process, finally I will, with divine help, walk again. My bodily functions are intact, including sight, hearing, sense of touch, and digestion. I am now learning to appreciate everything ten times over. Banal daily activities are no longer taken for granted, and I am grateful for the opportunity to perform them.

Beyond all these elements, the fact that I am alive is the greatest gift for me and my family. In recognition of this, I believe I will be able to endure all surgeries and medical treatments. Each event gives new meaning to my life. But this is not the place to go into details.

My dear friends, my talk has been long. Under normal circumstances it would now be your turn to ask questions and offer comments, but this time the conversation must be a monologue, although you can, of course, contact me or come to talk. It is important to me that you take with you the principles we have discussed. Be strong for the future and know that I shall always be ready to assist. You will be surprised at the high level you will be able to achieve and I believe with all my heart that you will do so.

I appreciate you all and am thinking of you,

Asael Lubotzky

In Memory of Amichai Merchavia

Amichai,

A bosom friend whom I shall never forget. Your image is etched in my consciousness: modest, deeply devout, a lover of the Torah; with an original, penetrating mind and profound spiritual strength; patriotic, a true friend, and a revered fighter and officer. No one could resist the compelling smile on your face, or your enchanting personality and purity of character.

All of these qualities were yours, each reflecting an aspect of your personality, but they are not enough – such elements do not reveal the whole. Your twenty-four years of life combined in a unique way Torah and *derekh eretz*, adherence to biblical precepts coupled with a modern way of life. You have been described as "gently tough": gentle to people and to your soldiers, yet as tough as a sturdy tree in faith and in strength against those who rise up against us.

Amichai, you fell leading your troops in a war to defend the country that you loved, sanctifying the Lord's name in public in a manner so suited to the words of Maimonides' *Laws of the Foundations of the Torah*:

These sanctified the holy name: Daniel, Hanania, Mishael and Azaria, Rabbi Akiva and his colleagues, and these were martyrs in the highest degree, of whom it is written: "for Thy sake are we killed all the day long; we are counted as sheep for the slaughter" (Ps.44:23) and "Gather My saints together unto Me; those that have made a covenant with Me by sacrifice." (Ps. 50:5)

Our acquaintance began in the Golani's base training camp. We enlisted in March 2003 in the unit for yeshiva students in the Fifty-First Battalion. Most of the soldiers came to basic training in groups from the various yeshivas, but you came on your own from Kedumim Yeshiva; yet, in a few days, you become involved in everything in the platoon, becoming a premier volunteer, from guard duties and drills to shouldering a stretcher or offering to stay at the base on Shabbat in place of a friend.

You were never afraid to speak up to commanders, yet your criticisms were always proffered with a pleasant smile, usually accompanied by a suggestion for improvement. In many cases, your comments arose from self-criticism, as you always demanded more from yourself than from others, so that your remarks were received with sympathy.

Some of the guard duties were paired and I was always glad to be your partner, knowing that I could expect two or more hours of fascinating, varied conversation: yeshiva life as contrasted with the army, the state of national-religious youth, the ideal image of a Jewish army, what can be improved in the company, how to strengthen the settlements, what halakhic insights we had learned about, and so forth.... Each item developed into an interesting discussion, and you were able to provide fresh insights on every issue. I always looked forward to these insights, as they emerged from wide knowledge, both religious and secular, and from deep original thought that analyzed events or trends in a broad context, penetrating beyond mere appearances.

In platoons composed of yeshiva students, there is often a tendency to be self-enclosed and not to open up to the rest of the company, but you saw great importance in making friends, often helping to make peace between the soldiers. You were always calm and serene, and when we ran into trouble, it was always you who put things into proportion. It was no surprise that you were appointed the Outstanding Soldier of the platoon at the conclusion of advanced training.

When we were moved to the outskirts of Ramallah, the accommodations we were given in the village of Eli was only a short distance from your family's home, and you frequently invited us, the members of the platoon, to your parents' house for Shabbat meals. Before one of the military operations, we were waiting in the briefing room for the arrival of the platoon commander, when you suddenly stood up and gave an overview of the Benjamin region. You loved the country and tried to imbue us all with your enthusiasm.

A week after we were moved to the border, the two of us received orders to patrol the area. We made our rounds in eight-hour shifts. Upon setting out, you took care to offer me suggestions: the points in the area to look out for, spectacular views not to be missed, villages in the sector that deserved to be visited, and so on…. You knew every detail of the landscape and your enthusiasm was contagious.

We enrolled together in a squad commanders' course. There, too, you were liked by everyone around. You were seen as a symbol, the perfect image of a Golani, reliable, loyal, and a true Zionist. You left for a period of study at Acre Yeshiva, and on your return were appointed commander of a squad of recruits in August 2004. From there, you went to officers' course.

At the end of the course you were assigned, in August 2005, to command a platoon of recruits in the Golani training base at Regavim. When I arrived to prepare the staff for the recruits of November 2005, you were just completing your task. We talked for hours, and I had much to learn from your experience. You told me about the extraordinary privilege you felt such a position offered: influencing people, dealing with human dilemmas, and learning how to take command. You explained how to focus on major elements and not be bogged down in details, and here, of course, you offered criticism of certain rules and obligations imposed from above, which, however, did not prevent you from performing your task admirably.

You called me one day to say that you had sent a letter to the chief of staff expressing your protest against the disengagement from

Gush Katif, executed by the IDF, and its further developments. You consulted me on how to act. After discussing the contents of the letter, I asked you what its purpose was – it was certainly not in the power of a single letter sent to the chief of staff to change the decree, while the move might prevent you, so I said, from fulfilling your aims. Your answer was typical: "There are situations in life when you have to tell the truth out loud, proclaim it, without weighing the pros and cons, without looking backward or forward, because it is the truth, and the truth is more important than any other consideration."

In the summer, we were transferred to the northern Gaza Strip, and spent a few weeks at Zikim, where we had more time to spend with each other. Again we found opportunities to discuss issues that so preoccupied you, and I was, as usual, happy to share my thoughts with you. We traveled north to the town of Bint Jbeil for Operation Steel Web. Its name was derived from Nasrallah's famous speech, "Spider's Web" which he delivered in that town after the IDF's withdrawal from Lebanon in 2000. Nasrallah's theory was that the Israeli home front was too weak to fight anymore. The soldiers' determination proved otherwise, displaying strength and courage in fierce battles in southern Lebanon that showed Israel to be strong. Amichai, you fell while leading your troops in an assault on the terrorists. Fire was opened on the Lead Platoon that you commanded, and you calmly set out with your troops to attack the terrorists from the side. It was a heroic battle in Bint Jbeil, where the battalion lost eight members. Your family, the Merchavia family, showed us, by its steadfastness, the path of faith and integrity. Despite their personal tragedy, your family, pioneers of Gush Emunim and Eli, continued to move ahead, standing tall in their faith.

My meeting with you in Lebanon, Amichai, was when you were no longer alive, in a funeral procession in which we returned the battalion's fallen across the border into the State of Israel.

We have been separated from your body, but your spirit continues to influence all who knew you. We gain strength from the memory of your character, and believe you have prepared us for the further challenges that await us. With the help of Heaven we shall succeed.

May your memory be blessed.

Acknowledgments

Without the people who helped me along the way, I could not have recovered from my injury, and certainly could not have written this book.

First, I wish to thank all those who participated in the military operation: the officers, commanders, and soldiers of the Golani, in general, and in particular of the Fifty-First Battalion, with whom I fought in Gaza and during the Second Lebanon War. Similarly, I wish to thank the many units of the IDF that fought with us. Their fighting spirit, friendship, and professionalism fostered a unique atmosphere, allowing me to focus on the fighting itself, knowing that the officers and their soldiers would do everything to ensure the success of the mission, including risking their lives. This is also the place to revere the memory of those who sacrificed themselves on the altar of the nation, including the ten from the Fifty-First Battalion who fell in the Second Lebanon War: Roi Klein, Alex Shwartsman, Amichai Merchavia, Idan Cohen, Shimon Dahan, Ohad Klauzner, Shimon Adega, Assaf Namer, Yosef Abutbul, and Tamer (Tomer) Amer.

Special thanks are due to the commanders and fighters of my company, Company B, for a partnership that lasted throughout the campaign, especially the soldiers and commanders of the Third Platoon, for placing their trust in me and for the privilege of commanding them. I thank them also for the support, the visits, and the phone calls after my injury.

I should like to express my gratitude to the following:

To the members of my company, along with those from Company B of the Fifty-Third Battalion of the Barak Brigade, who rescued me and my comrades after the attack.

To the medical staff who raced to the border to treat me, and for the life-saving treatment they provided.

To the medical teams at Rambam Hospital for their dedication during the war in general, and for the sensitivity, care, humanity, and professional treatment they provided. To the departments of intensive care, orthopedics and plastic surgery, whose staff made every effort to make my stay with them as pleasant as possible. To Dr. Alex Lerner, the orthopedic surgeon who treated me on the first night, for his courageous and successful decision to save my leg, his devoted care, and his skill as a surgeon. His encouragement, and his faith in the success of his treatment gave me inspiration and strength.

To the medical personnel of Tel Hashomer Hospital, where I underwent a series of operations and prolonged hospitalization. Its departments of plastic surgery and orthopedic rehabilitation, for their staff's professionalism, support, and encouragement.

To the many members of my family and of other groups who visited and supported me and my family in difficult times; and the friends who spent long hours with me, stayed in the hospital with me overnight and for Shabbat, providing stimulating conversation, with encouragement and great devotion. And to the rabbis and students from the high-school yeshiva Neve Shmuel and the Hesder yeshiva Birkat Moshe in Ma'ale Adumim for their many visits, concern, and prayers for my health and wellbeing.

To the wounded soldiers I came to know during long hospitalizations, for the bond of solidarity, and for their sense of fun and optimism. The lengthy discussions and encouragement, their humor and openness helped me face that period more directly and honestly.

To the bereaved families whose steadfastness strengthened my spirit, and with special thanks to the family of my dear friend Amichai Merchavia, to Moshe and Tova and their children, who opened their hearts and home to me, allowing me to study Torah and continue in the path of Amichai. And to Moshe for his great assistance in the description of the battle in Bint Jbeil.

To those good people, the volunteers who came to be with the wounded, cheering us with their help all the way: Hulda Gurevich, Yaakov Selavan, Revital Turjeman, Revital Ozeri, Assaf Halevi, Carmel Shiloni, Tal Fadlon, Malkiel Lerner, Dalia Shats, Hana Greenwald, Yehudit Hason, Sarah Zelcerman, Simone Farbstein, and many others who came to visit and brought food, joy, and many happy surprises.

To the Golani Casualties Department for the support, sensitivity, and care shown to bereaved families and to the wounded. Their female officers and commanders were there from the start, supplying empathy and support to my parents when I was in intensive care, giving me a further reason to be proud of belonging to the family of the Golani Brigade. Also to the contact officers for the wounded, for help during hospitalization in organizing family accommodation, travel, and permits, always with a pleasant smile.

To the staff of the Defense Ministry's Rehabilitation Department, who accompanied and helped me and my family during the lengthy hospitalization and rehabilitation process.

To the Army's Disabled Veterans Organization, Brothers for Life, Tikvot, and OneFamily for support and encouragement.

My thanks to those who urged me to write this book, reading drafts, offering comments, and making significant contributions to style and content. To Professor Simcha Goldin for the push and the encouragement to write and document the war events from the perspective of a fighter in the field. To Dr. Eden Hacohen for the initial encouragement and for his acute linguistic and literary advice. To Chavi Kraus for her brilliant comments uncovering ideas on many levels. To Mickey Schonfeld for helpful advice and guidance in processing significant points. To the editor, Dr. Tali Vishne, for understanding my world, enlightening me on many points, all with unparalleled speed and efficiency, and to Dov Eichenwald, the general director of *Yediot Sfarim*, my Hebrew publisher, for his generous support throughout the process.

To Dr. Guita Wilf, for instigating the English translation of the book. To my dear grandfather, Professor Murray Roston, for his professional and loving translation of the text. To Toby Press, for its meticulous and hard work in publishing the English edition; to the publisher, Matthew Miller, and editor in chief, Gila Fine, for their faith in this project, and to the talented editors Tomi Mager, Avigayil Steiglitz, Suzi Libenson, and Ezra Margulies.

Lastly – and most significantly – to my family. To my many relatives, especially my immediate family, for their support and love. To my parents, who raised and educated me, and implanted in me the faith and optimism to overcome the challenges that faced me. My parents, my brothers, and my sisters were with me from the beginning, a devotion that knows no boundaries, sympathy and love without end, always close to my bed, ready to do everything to help me and make life easier. They also contributed greatly to the writing of this book: encouraging me, raising points, offering comments and insights with repeated readings of the various drafts.

To my dear wife Avital, who joined me on my journey after my injury, though it seems as if she's always been there. Thank you for your strength, your faith, and the joy of raising our children Neta Ruth, Naveh Amichai, and Yuval Iser.

Thank you.

About the Author

Asael Lubotzky was born in Jerusalem in 1983 and grew up in the town of Efrat. He studied at the Hesder Yeshiva in Ma'ale Adumim, before enlisting in the IDF, where he served as platoon commander in the Fifty-First Battalion of the Golani Brigade. Lubotzky led his troops fighting in Gaza and Lebanon, until his severe injury in the Second Lebanon War. Following a lengthy and difficult rehabilitation, he took up studies at the Hebrew University Hadassah Medical School, and today works as a physician at Shaare Zedek Medical Center Jerusalem. In addition, Lubotzky addresses IDF units, as well as groups from Israel and abroad, on the subjects of Zionism, courage, and fortitude. He lives in Jerusalem, is married to Avital, and has three children.

The fonts used in this book are from the Garamond family

The Toby Press publishes fine writing
on subjects of Israel and Jewish interest.
For more information, visit www.tobypress.com.